Mis-directing the Play

Mis-directing the Play

AN ARGUMENT AGAINST
CONTEMPORARY THEATRE

Terry McCabe

Ivan R. Dee

CHICAGO

Library of Congress Cataloging-in-Publication Data:
McCabe, Terry.
    Mis-directing the play : an argument against contemporary theatre / Terry McCabe.
        p.   cm.
    Includes index.
    ISBN 1-56663-353-2 (alk. paper)
    1. Theater—Production and direction.   2. Drama—Explication.
    I. Title.

PN2053 .M393 2001
792'.0233—dc21   00-066034

This book is dedicated to my family—

Nancy Flowers, Hazel Flowers-McCabe, and Tyler Flowers-McCabe

—and to everyone who worked at Stormfield Theatre in Chicago

between the spring of 1983 and the fall of 1987

Contents

Preface

IF WE COULD first know *where* we are, and *whither* we are tending, we could then better judge *what* to do, and *how* to do it." Lincoln was talking about something far more important than directing plays, but his words sum up the mood and, I hope, the approach of this book. I wrote it in an attempt to clarify—for myself as much as for anyone who might read it—the issue at the heart of the director's job in today's theatre: Does the director *determine* what the play means, or does the director *discover* what the play means?

I first became aware of this issue when JoAnne Akalaitis directed Samuel Beckett's *Endgame* for the American Repertory Theatre in 1984 and set off the most public debate that the question of directorial liberty has yet received.

Endgame is the story of Hamm who cannot stand up and Clov who cannot sit down. They are in a room with two windows and not much else, and they are playing their endgame. Akalaitis set the play's action in a New York City subway station, seemingly after a nuclear holocaust aboveground. This gave the production a geographical specificity and a political subtext that the play itself lacks. Beckett heard about the production and sought a court order to shut it down.

American Repertory negotiated a settlement that allowed its production to go on, but it was required to include in its stagebill a program note written by Beckett condemning the show. Here's the key paragraph:

Any production of *Endgame* which ignores my stage directions is completely unacceptable to me. My play requires an empty room and two small windows. The American Repertory Theatre production which dismisses my directions is a complete parody of the play as conceived by me. Anybody who cares for the work couldn't fail to be disgusted by this.

This quickly became the most widely read author's note ever written for a play program.

Opposite it, American Repertory printed a response by its artistic director, Robert Brustein, which said in part:

To threaten any deviations from a purist rendering of this or any other play—to insist on strict adherence to each parenthesis of the published text—not only robs collaborating artists of their interpretive freedom but threatens to turn the theatre into a waxworks.

The sides could not be more clearly drawn, and the territory of this book could not be better mapped.

Brustein does not quite play fair (the concern that launched Beckett's legal action was not "strict adherence to each parenthesis" but the complete physical aspect of his play), but his point is not frivolous. He is right if the object of directing is to make the director's vision of the material clear to an audience. If such is the case, to suppress the free flight of the director's imagination is indeed to call for a dead theatre.

He is wrong if, as this book argues, the object of directing is rather to make clear the director's best sense of what the playwright had in mind. If this is the case, a director whose production is denounced by the playwright has failed: if my job is to express your meaning, and you say I got it wrong, then I got it wrong. The theatre of such a director may not be a waxworks, but it is not exactly living either. It is the undead: capable of independent movement and speech, but without the soul its creator intended for it.

Beckett may have won the battle—in the seventeen years since he went to court, as far as I can ascertain, Akalaitis has yet to direct another of his plays—but his side is losing the war. Over the same years, the approach to directing that disgusted him has become less and less controversial. Increasingly it is coming to define what it is that a director does.

As I write this I have in front of me a negative review for a revisionist production of *Desire Under the Elms* staged a few months ago. The critic is at pains to catalogue what he calls the director's "wrong-headed decisions" in the execution of the concept, but he never questions the idea of approaching the play with a revisionist concept in the first place. To the contrary, he endorses it by writing that "this [concept] creates a tantalyzing new way of presenting" the play, before going on to say he doesn't think it works in any of its particulars. Never does he contemplate the possibility that the play might have been better off if done the way Eugene O'Neill wrote it.

This possibility is ignored because it has become an article of faith that a play is about what the director chooses to have it be about. At one point in his review, the critic writes that the director's decision to cast the family interracially "has further emphasized" the play's "culural conflict." But there is no specifically cultural conflict in O'Neill's play, for the family in conflict is written to be of the same race and social background. What the critic saw was not something the director had "further emphasized" but had created out of whole cloth. The assumption underlying Brustein's defense of Akalaitis—that the play is a found object to be reshaped to express the director's concerns—now dominates the field.

The biggest help with the book came from friends and colleagues who read drafts of various portions and offered observations and criticisms. The two who did the most in this regard were Kristine Thatcher and Sheldon Patinkin. Neither of them is known among their friends for having copious free time, but they never hesitated to respond in detail to something I had written, and the book is better than it would have been if I hadn't had them to lean on. I can't thank them enough.

Valuable feedback was also provided by Nancy Beckett, Pauline

Brailsford, James Glossman, Andrew Meyers, Tom Mula, Kathy O'Malley, Mary Poole, and Douglas Post. They are responsible for many improvements in the book; the flaws remain mine.

A number of others helped in important ways. Above all I am grateful to Nancy Flowers for untold kindnesses. Joan Henslee provided invaluable research material that lifted the whole book; Cameron Feagin, Eddie Jemison, and Jamie Pachino each brought useful information to my attention. Certain actors shared stories with me about difficult situations with directors, and to show my gratitude I will not name them here.

The books that helped me define what the ambitions of my book might be were not about theatre, but about individual perspectives on complicated subjects that the authors loved: Greil Marcus's *Mystery Train,* C. S. Lewis's *An Experiment in Criticism,* a collection of George Orwell's essays carrying the hard-to-argue-with title *A Collection of Essays,* James Herndon's *How to Survive in Your Native Land,* and Garry Wills's books in general.

I am grateful to my students at Columbia College for the opportunity to try out some of the ideas in the book in class, and to three teachers of mine who helped me care about the craft of making myself clear on paper: Beth Campen, Eugene Bristow, and Linda Jenkins. Finally, my editor and publisher, Ivan Dee, has been both patient and eagle-eyed, which is an excellent combination.

"I do not try to be generous or fair," Paul Goodman once wrote, "but I have seen what I am talking about and I hope I am rational." Well, I couldn't put it any better than that. What I have seen is a theatre drifting toward decadence. I have no illusions that anything I say will reverse this drift, but I do hope my book can be useful to the discussion.

It may be that any generation gets the theatre it deserves, and that our theatre is decadent because our times are decadent. Even so, by beginning to understand the difference between the way it is and the way it's supposed to be, we resist the drifting and perhaps start to deserve a better theatre.

I'm very definite about what I want to do,

but at the same time I'm most pleased, in the end,

when nobody knows I've been there.

—Alan Schneider

MYRA: Is it really that good? His first play?

SIDNEY: It can't miss. A gifted director couldn't even hurt it.

—Ira Levin, *Deathtrap*

Mis-directing the Play

1 : The Myth of the Director

Not long ago, a celebrated production of *Hamlet* featured, at the play's most famous moment, Hamlet spray-painting on a wall

TO BE / NOT TO BE

and then turning out to the audience and saying, "That is the question." Relating this later to an interviewer, the director congratulated himself on the choice: "It exploded the play in this wonderful way: everybody just laughed and got over it in a perfect symbiotic relationship."*

But what, precisely, is this moment in the theatre about? Surely the moment as staged is not about the play, not about the character's struggle at this point in the action. It is impossible to believe that

---

*From Arthur Bartow, *The Director's Voice: Twenty-One Interviews* (New York, 1988). The publisher, Theatre Communications Group, is the national service organization for the not-for-profit professional theatre, and many of the directors interviewed are artistic directors of TCG's member theatres. As a result the book sometimes reads like a Chamber of Commerce guide to local restaurants: all are good. Nonetheless it provides an interesting cross-section of directors (including most of the celebrated *auteurs* of the day) talking about what they do and how they go about it. My favorite comment in the book is from anti-*auteur* Gregory Mosher, explaining his minimalist approach to staging: "I really like it when shifting your weight onstage is a big deal."

Shakespeare intends the line to get a laugh. The audience laughs because it has stepped outside the play to admire the cleverness of the director.

Radical reinterpretation, even reshaping, of dramatic texts is the big story in stage directing over the last few decades. The position of the director in the theatre—a job which was invented in only the last 125 of the theatre's 2,500 years of recorded history—has arrived at a point of central prominence, so even the play itself is frequently little more than a found object, with which the director combines other production elements to form his or her own theatrical statement. Many of the best-known American directors today—undeniably talented artists such as JoAnne Akalaitis and Peter Sellars—have built their reputations on just such an approach to directing. Many other directors who don't go as far as these two would nonetheless agree with them that it is the director who controls the play in production. One writer for a national theatre service organization describes the modern director approvingly this way: "Today, the director is even more firmly in command and frequently becomes the initiator, using *text*, music and visuals *as colors in the directorial palette*" (emphases added).

The premise of this book is simple: directing that seeks to control the text, instead of subordinating itself to the text, is bad directing. I believe the director's job is to tell the playwright's story as clearly and as interestingly as possible. Period.

If you are a director, your power in the theatre is such that it can be relatively easy to bend the play so that it fulfills some other purpose you have defined. It is, after all, your vision of the play that unites the production. You have ultimate control over all the show's elements. The other participating artists may well make vital contributions, but even the question of vitality is answered by you: those contributions that you feel enhance your interpretation are declared valuable and are incorporated; those that you feel deviate from it are cut.

Given these facts, it is understandable that the line between serving the play and making it serve you can be blurred. After all, a bold reimagining of a given play can reinvigorate it and bring it home to the audience fresher and more powerful than ever. But the danger lies in how easy it is to have the audience's evening in the theatre be about the boldness, and not about the play. It's not always easy to see where the line between the two lies, but one thing seems sure: a tragic hero contemplating suicide should not get a laugh.

The myth of the theatre director is that he or she is the *auteur* of what happens on the stage, just as the film director is the *auteur* of what we see on the screen. The myth is not true — cannot be true — and belief in the myth leads to bad directing and is therefore destructive of good theatre.

The film director is properly considered the *auteur* of the film, its controlling intelligence and thus its true author, because the director stands at the point of intersection between the film and the audience. Film is a director's medium because the person filling that role makes the moment-to-moment decisions as to precisely what the audience will see and hear: from which angles to film, whether to shoot in close-up, which take to use, and so on. A film audience sees and hears only what the director selects for them.

Live theatre, an actor's medium, doesn't work that way. The person who stands at the point of intersection between the play and the audience is the actor. The defining characteristic of live theatre, of course, is that it is slightly different every night, precisely because it is performed by live actors each time as if for the first time. The cast, not the director, is the play's delivery system. From performance to performance, unexpected nuances emerge, meanings deepen, actions become more specific. The director controls none of this: moment-to-moment decisions as to what the audience will see and hear are made by the actors in the course of each performance. This is neither good nor bad. It is simply the nature of the beast: live performance is the art form of the live performer.

Stage directors who attempt to be *auteurs* of the theatre are denying the nature of their art form. And so they give us productions that depend heavily upon "nonlive" elements such as videotape, recorded music, and elaborate technical effects. So they give us four-hour productions of plays that can be read out loud at a comfortable pace in two and a half. They give us productions that are about the directing, not about the play. They do all this because they are caught up in a myth that does not describe their reality. They should be making movies.

This is not to say that the idea of a director reimagining a play is wrong. Not at all; it is what all directors must do each time they direct. No play comes to life just by being staged. Some plays get produced thousands of times; each good production is good because its director has imagined it as a specific, unique living thing. The distinction to be made is whether the director's imagining provides the audience with a new avenue into what the playwright has to say, or whether the director reduces the play to raw material to be shaped into what the director has to say. A look at two famous productions may make this distinction clear.

Tadashi Suzuki's sublime production of *The Trojan Women* is set in a Japanese city at the end of World War II. A woman sits in a cemetery. Her family is dead, her possessions are gone except for a handful of items she has carried here. To help herself through her pain, the woman thinks about the characters in Euripides' play, and we see her live through their struggles as she enacts their story. The present-tense theatrical reality is that of 1945 Japan; the drama that unfolds is that of ancient Troy. The woman's body is inhabited by the spirits of the individual women of Troy. The characters are not played by separate actresses in this production but are channeled, one at a time, by Suzuki's actress, the great Kayoko Shiraishi. An astonishing moment in the production, and one that defines its approach, is the transformation of the woman from Hecuba to Cassandra. All she does is stand and remove her black kimono, revealing a white one underneath, but in the moment she goes from being an old woman to a young girl, from being heavy and weary with loss to being poised on the edge of a knife. Later, Andromache is raped, and her son Astyanax (represented by a cloth doll) is ripped apart onstage. Hecuba binds the child's severed arm to his body with her sash and covers the corpse with cloth. The woman, no longer one of Euripides' characters but now Euripidean in her own right, packs up her few belongings. In the play's final section, she berates Jizo, the Buddhist deity who is traditionally the Protector of Children, who has stood silently onstage since the beginning of the play, seeing everything and doing nothing.

Suzuki has taken enormous liberties here. Aside from the setting and the central device of having the woman portray multiple characters, he has also altered key events in the play. Euripides does not have Andromache raped, nor does he have Astyanax killed onstage. Suzuki has replaced the play's opening scene between Poseidon and Athena, the gods Euripides indicts for Troy's devastation, with the silent presence of Jizo throughout the action. And he has completely eliminated the one scene in the original play that ties the action to the details of the Trojan War, the confrontation between Menelaus and Helen.

None of this matters. The fundamental truth of Suzuki's production is the fundamental truth of Euripides' play. This is so because Suzuki did not take *The Trojan Women* as a means of making a comment on Hiroshima and Nagasaki. The reverse is the case: Suzuki's production takes his country's agony as a reason to examine the universality of *The Trojan Women*. This modern Japanese woman explores an ancient Greek play as a means of transcending her own situation, and so she takes us with her. She moves outside herself into Euripides' tragedy. Because this is the action Suzuki gives us, his production is about the play: its subject is not the director's opinion of Japan's defeat but the playwright's compassion for those at whose cost victories are won. This is what *The Trojan Women* should be about, no matter where it is set or how it is done, which is why this production works. As with any great work of art, Suzuki's *Trojan Women* presents a set of specifics, which it transcends to achieve universality.

Contrast this with what might be the most famous American "concept production" ever done, Orson Welles's groundbreaking 1937 production of *Julius Caesar*. By all accounts an exciting and bracing evening in the theatre, it is also clear that the production was designed to fit Shakespeare's play into the director's concept.

Where Suzuki had taken care not to put the ancient Greek play into modern Japan in literal terms—his audience was not given a cast of Japanese characters with Greek names, but rather a Japanese character who reimagined an ancient Greek story in personal terms—Welles simply recast Shakespeare's Rome as Mussolini's: jackboots, modern uniforms, a musical score that quoted from fascist Italy's anthem. The play was made to work as a parable about the European dictators then moving the world toward war. Welles's biographer Simon Callow points out that this focus "meant that a great deal of the political complexity of the play was sacrificed. . . ." He might have added that a great deal of the play's *dramatic* complexity is sacrificed by a concept that says, in effect, that the play can mean only this one thing. Welles's concept depended on keeping Brutus the sole focus; toward this end, he eliminated most of the role of Mark Antony, cut or greatly reduced certain other characters, streamlined the individuality out of the Roman mob, and at one point substituted some lines from *Coriolanus* that better suited his purposes. It is not simply that Welles edited the script extensively; Suzuki's alterations of Euripides are as extensive, and I have no complaint about them. Welles's changes would be fine too if they were done to provide a fresh route into Shakespeare's play.

Such seems not to have been the case, however, judging from the reviews. Mary McCarthy wrote bitterly, "The production of *Caesar* turns into a battleground between Mr. Welles's play and Shakespeare's play. . . . If the classics are to play an important role in the American theatre, their contents ought at least to be examined." Most other reviews were favorable but came around to the same admission. John Mason Brown raved about the production but allowed that "the play ceases to be Shakespeare's tragedy. . . ." Brooks Atkinson's review was favorable but described the show as "modern variations on the theme of Shakespeare's *Julius Caesar*."

The difference between this production and Suzuki's is that Welles does not allow his audience to establish its own connections to the play. If you and I are in his audience, whatever associations we might otherwise bring to *Caesar* are short-circuited by the director, who has made it clear that—at least for this evening—the play is only about a topic that Shakespeare cannot possibly have had in mind. To Welles, the script is as meat to the sausage maker: when he's done, the sausage bears little resemblance to the meat he fed into the grinder. Welles's *Caesar* is his theatrical statement about 1930s Europe; it limits the play. Suzuki's *Trojan Women* is his theatrical statement about Euripides' tragedy; it opens the play up. A world of difference lies between the two.

Creative is a word that gets bandied about casually, as an approximate synonym for *artistic*. Strictly speaking, there is only one creative artist in the theatre. It is the playwright, the only one who makes something out of nothing. The rest of us—directors, designers, actors—are interpretive artists. We take what the playwright has created and demonstrate to an audience what we think the playwright's creation looks and sounds like.

This demonstration, not the play itself, is what the director must control. The number of different artists working on a production requires a central organizing principle. Otherwise, if there are twenty people working on a show there will be twenty different demonstrations going on, and the show will be a mess. A unified production requires an ongoing conversation among the people putting the show together, in order to ensure that everyone is proceeding from the same principle and working toward the same goal.

A director's proper function in the production of a play is to begin the conversation and then to guide that conversation to a coherent finish. "This is what I think happens in the play, and this is what I think that action means." The ability to make a clear and concise statement of this nature about a play is the essence of the director's art.

We are told over and over that theatre is the most collaborative of arts; less frequently pointed out is that the director is generally the only person who collaborates personally with each contributor to a production. To a certain degree, in fact, the other individual collaborators are unaware of the precise contributions of some of their fellows until the work is seen onstage. The playwright, if present at all, may have little or no contact with, say, the lighting designer. The set designer may have next to no interaction with the cast, and so on. But the director collaborates with everyone.

The director stands between clarity and confusion onstage, bringing focus to what would otherwise be a disjointed collaboration. His or her tools in this endeavor are two: the ability to understand the action of the play in its essential form, and the ability to make that action and its meaning uniformly clear to the disparate group of artists working on the show.

The modern director who distorts the play is no better than Nahum Tate, Collee Cibber, or any of the other seventeenth-century manglers of Shakespeare's tragedies who substituted happy endings of their own devising for the tragic ones the playwright had thought sufficient. In their improved version of *Romeo and Juliet*, the play's final catastrophe is averted and the lovers survive. So does Cordelia in their corrected *King Lear*—and she marries Edgar and they go on to rule Britain together. These changes were made in order to—as the changers saw it—make the plays relevant to the audiences of their day. On one level they appear to have succeeded: their versions held the stage for a century and a half. But today we feel that their work violated the plays.

The day may arrive when we feel the same way about, for instance, JoAnne Akalaitis setting *Endgame* in a cluttered subway station complete with a train, puddles of water, and rubble, despite the stage direction with which Samuel Beckett begins his script: "Bare interior."

This book is an attempt to hurry that day along. It explores the questions of directing a play: analyzing a play's dramatic action and coming to a director's decisions about the script, and implementing those decisions in the director's work with designers and actors. It argues that a correct relationship between the director and the play must in turn affect the way a good director works with actors. It touches on related issues, such as the ethics of running an audition and why the director shouldn't work with a dramaturg, and so on. Throughout the book, the focus is on shedding the counterproductive myth of the modern stage director as creative *auteur*, and urging in its place a return to first principles: the idea of the director as the interpretive artist in charge of putting the playwright's play onstage.

2 : "Tyranny is always weakness."

—James Russell Lowell

IF YOU BELIEVE that your job as director is to fashion the production so that the play reflects your artistic vision, then you are not only bad, you are dangerous. That is to say: the oppression of the actor is a logical corollary to the idea that the director is the center of the theatre.

An imaginative director who subordinates him- or herself to the play—a good director—sees the actors and designers as valuable colleagues precisely because they might enlarge the director's own sense of the play. On the other hand, the director who sees other people's work as colors in the directorial palette can only control and manipulate the play by controlling and manipulating their contributions. The *auteur* is not only more likely to behave like the martinet, he or she *must* do so.*

*Some theatre practitioners take the deconstructionist view that all meaning is arbitrary, that it is not possible for anyone to know another's mind. Therefore it is impossible, they say, for a director to understand a playwright's intention in any real sense, and so a director must—not may, but must—use the play for self-expression, as that is the only expression possible.

Why on earth are these people in theatre in the first place? The whole art form is based on the idea that it *is* possible to imagine what it's like to be some-

It is a few years ago, during one of the periodic national debates over government funding of the arts. Des McAnuff, not yet the refashioner of The Who's *Tommy*, a record album, into *The Who's Tommy*, a Broadway musical, is artistic director of the La Jolla Playhouse and one of the hottest directors in the country. He is about to open his production of *Twelfth Night* to rave reviews, including its beatification by *Time* as one of the nation's ten best shows of the year. The production is McAnuff's statement on the arts funding controversy.

Shakespeare's comedy is at first glance an unlikely vessel in which to carry this particular water. *Twelfth Night* is about Viola, a young woman who is shipwrecked in Illyria, disguises herself as a man, and enters the service of the duke Orsino. She falls in love with Orsino, who is lovesick over the countess Olivia, who falls in love with the disguised Viola. By play's end, Orsino is paired off with the now undisguised Viola, and Olivia with Viola's twin brother Sebastian, whom she finds equally satisfactory.

This story has as little to do with the question of arts funding as with the twelfth night of Christmas. But the play also features one of Shakespeare's best-known subplots, and it is here that McAnuff finds his point of entry. He conceives Malvolio, Olivia's chief of staff, to suggest Senator Jesse Helms, the right wing's most buffoonish opponent of arts funding. Malvolio's running battle with the fun-loving members of Olivia's household is McAnuff's version of the fight over arts funding: Olivia's uncle and the rest live off her largesse but contribute nothing to the household that Malvolio is capable of appreciating; he despises them for this and seeks to expel them, but they expose him as a hypocrite and make him a laughingstock.

one else. If you believe that an actress *can* play Medea, and that an audience *can* be moved by her performance, then you have no excuse for not realizing that a director *can* understand what Euripides is after.

No two of the countless directors who attempt to know Euripides' mind will agree completely with each other, just as no good director's actual production ever lives up to his or her ideal production. But to use this fact as an excuse for not making the attempt is plain artistic quackery.

This is one type of directorial concept: elements of the play are interpreted as a metaphor for an issue or event that exists outside the play, and the production is organized around that metaphor. One test of whether a concept works is how it resonates with the rest of the play, the parts that did not suggest the metaphor in the first place. If, say, a production of *Othello* were to use the O. J. Simpson murder case as its concept, the concept wouldn't work because it makes no allowance for Iago. The central relationship in that play is not between the black man and the white woman he kills in a fit of jealousy, but between him and his most trusted confidante, the only person whose lies could have turned Othello against Desdemona. An approach to *Othello* that grounds the relationship between Othello and Desdemona in an understanding of that between Simpson and his slain ex-wife misses the core of the play. It gives us an Othello who wouldn't need to be tricked into killing his wife, an Othello with no tragic dimension.

Does Malvolio as Jesse Helms work for *Twelfth Night*? It doesn't cohere in any way with the play's main story, of course, but even in the context of the subplot, the concept seems problematic. If Malvolio is Helms, then Malvolio's chief nemesis—the aptly named Sir Toby Belch—would seem to represent the arts community. But he is a drunken, gluttonous lout, and his fellow recipient of Malvolio's wrath, Sir Andrew Aguecheek, is feeble, cowardly, and simple-minded. They are funny in their foolishness, and Malvolio is certainly a hypocrite, but is that really the case for continued arts funding?

Of course, the real test of a production concept is how it works in performance, so let us examine what the audience saw. The production was celebrated for two things: the director's political view of the play's subplot, and his extravagant visual style. *Time*'s year-end tribute, to cite the show's highest praise, mentioned nothing but these two elements.

The two go hand in hand when the director's theme is not the play's. How else to inject a theme that is not in the action than to put visual metaphors onstage?

The set—any production's chief metaphor for its theme—was

an immense *faux*-marble museum lobby: white floor except for a center rectangle with a mirrored surface, walls of gray marble, all resting atop a flight of stairs as wide as the stage. Giant glass display cases were prominently located on either side of the stage, and various items were displayed in them in the course of the evening. The debate that was McAnuff's inspiration centered on funding by the National Endowment of the Arts of controversial museum exhibits, and so he defined the play's universe by suggesting a museum as the arena of conflict.

None of the objects displayed in the glass cases during the performance were involved in the action in any direct way, but each was a visual metaphor of one sort or another. A giant stuffed bear was displayed during the scene wherein Malvolio has been imprisoned and is being taunted, an apparent reference to Elizabethan bear-baiting. The lower half of a mannikin was displayed at one point, wearing yellow cross-gartered tights that appeared to some to have been strategically stuffed; this seemed to relate to the play's issue of cross-gender disguise in some way, as well as referring to Malvolio's humiliation. Displayed at various other moments were a red-and-white electric guitar (rebellious art, perhaps?), sixteenth-century armor (outdated rigidity?), and something that one reviewer took for "the spitting image of Molière." At one point a refrigerator, open and fully stocked, was suspended in the air over a scene being played.

This parade of metaphors took place behind the actors, or off to the sides, or above them. At no time did any of them acknowledge any of it. It was never a part of their action, which means it was by definition a distraction from it. When the refrigerator appeared in the air, or the bear appeared in the glass case, some fraction of an audience member's attention was given over to wondering, "What's this and how does it fit into the play?" This reaction was inevitable and therefore undoubtedly intended by the director. Fine, but the attention given in this way was taken from the actors. The play's action, which is in the hands of the actors, was deemphasized by a directorial choice that entertains by means of sleight-of-hand rather than by storytelling.

Something similar happened with the costumes. The costume design was eclectically anachronistic. Some of the clothes were from the twentieth century, others from the sixteenth. Some characters wore some from each. In his cross-gartered scene, for instance, wherein Shakespeare has been specific about clothing, Malvolio wore Elizabethan clothes, but elsewhere he wore a modern three-piece suit.

This approach to the costumes served the political nature of the concept by creating the impression that all time periods coexist in one great synchrony. As ideas extraneous to *Twelfth Night* go, this one is at least interesting. But, again, every moment the audience spends encountering this idea is attention away from what the actors are doing. A good costume is an *expression of* the character who wears it; if instead it is a *comment on* the character, we notice the comment more than we do the character. The point of Malvolio's modern suit was to underline the contemporary parallel McAnuff was making; all the national press coverage on the show that I have seen mentioned McAnuff's Malvolio-as-Jesse-Helms metaphor, but none named the actor who actually played the role.

Throughout the performance, visual spectacle abounded. Changing vistas of sea and sky were projected intermittently. A shower of tennis balls cascaded onto the stage at one point. Little of this spectacle appears to have had much to do with the actors' performances, and occasionally it seems to have hampered them. In one scene Sir Toby and Fabian are talking when Maria enters hurriedly to tell them to come see Malvolio making a fool of himself. McAnuff set this scene in a steambath, complete with steam. The steam made the mirrored part of the floor slippery, and a cast member reports that it happened more than once in performance that the actress playing Maria slipped and fell when making her running entrance.

Indeed, dealing with the set and its tricks was apparently enough of an ordeal that mishaps were not rare. One of the show's few negative reviews, written by a San Diego *Gay Times* critic who saw the show later in its run, described the cast as "so tired that . . . actors tripped, got caught in set pieces, and dropped their props."

Sometimes, in the name of visual interest, stage business was added that seems to have hampered the scene being played. Viola's first scene with Orsino is a delicate one. She is disguised as the fictional Cesario and is being sent by Orsino to woo Olivia on his behalf. She must show us that she has herself fallen in love with Orsino while concealing it from him; he must show that he has established a real intimacy with Cesario without seeming to perceive his servant's true nature. McAnuff set the scene at the beach; upstage of Orsino and Viola/Cesario were two of Orsino's other attendants, who tossed a brightly colored beachball back and forth during the scene's dialogue. A cast member tells me that when the actors playing Orsino and Viola complained during rehearsals that the subtleties of the scene were being upstaged by this distracting business, McAnuff agreed to compromise—and directed the attendants to toss the ball less frequently.

In one respect, even issues of casting seem to have been resolved in favor of visual quirkiness over dramatic logic. Women were cast as Valentine and Curio, two of Orsino's male attendants, and then put in male attire and even given mustaches. Was the audience supposed to accept them as male characters? If so, it didn't happen, as any number of reviewers pointed out. Or was the audience supposed to understand that these two were women who had, long before Viola came up with the very same idea, disguised themselves as men and entered Orsino's service? The notion is bizarre but unavoidable. If McAnuff's Illyria is a place where it is not all that unusual for a woman to disguise herself as a man, then Viola's decision to do so is trivialized. It lessens her cleverness and her chutzpah; it eliminates her uniqueness.

And what of the women playing Valentine and Curio? What are their characters up to? Are they in love with Orsino too? Do they just need the jobs? Are they in league with each other, or do they not even know the other is a woman? Do they see through Viola's disguise? If so, why do they keep quiet about it? All these are inevitable acting questions, but of course the play gives no opportunity for the answers to be played.

Chekhov said there is no reason to bring a gun onstage in Act

One unless it's going to be fired in Act Three; that is to say, don't set up an audience expectation that you're not going to fulfill. By having Curio, Valentine, and Cesario all be women in male attire, McAnuff brought three guns onstage, only one of which he had any plans to shoot. This is a disservice to the actors who have to enact the director's choice every night.

For it is frequently the actors who are blamed when the director ignores the play in favor of the production. When impressive displays of spectacle pull the audience's attention away from the action, it can seem that the actors are less than compelling. This appears to have happened with McAnuff's *Twelfth Night*, judging from the reviews.

In general, critics heaped praise on the show's visual style and gave short shrift to the actors. The *Los Angeles Times* set the tone by calling the actors the show's "weakest elements," and described the production as "a director's confection—distinguished more for the way McAnuff has manipulated his strings than the individual contributions of his players." The *L.A. Weekly* called the technical designs "spectacular," but the best it could say for the cast was that they were "game." One of the smaller local papers called the set "the true star" of the show. *Time* named the production among the year's ten best without feeling the need to praise a single performance in it.

Were the actors in fact bad? There is no reason to think so. Certainly McAnuff thought they were good when he cast them, and the show's program lists both an East Coast casting director and a West Coast casting director, so he had a national talent pool from which to draw. And the cast's program biographies list impressive credits from Broadway, off-Broadway, and important resident theatres across the country, evidence of flourishing careers in a highly competitive profession. No, it seems these were perfectly good actors, disfranchised by their director and done in by his nationally acclaimed production.

Here's a funnier story. A production of *The Three Sisters*, staged at a lesser-known theatre by a lesser-known director, was set in a graveyard. The *play* is set in the home of Olga, Masha, and Irina Prozorov, but this production of it was set in a graveyard. Were the sisters supposed to be living in the graveyard? "I guess so," one of the cast members told me some time after the show had closed, in a tone that suggested he was still a little puzzled by the matter. "We sat on tombstones and had tea."

Two days before opening, the final visual element was added: the set was blanketed with dead leaves. This is another type of concept: thematic metaphors, in this case of death and decay, are made concrete and substituted for the physical world of the play described in the text. The object is, I suppose, to make the theme clearer. Incidentally, there were no trees in this graveyard, merely a blanketing of leaves. Verisimilitude sometimes takes a back seat when a production concept is driving.

The actors soon discovered a problem that might have been foreseen: dead leaves crunch when you walk through them. And so the director discovered he had trouble hearing lines delivered while actors were moving through leaves. The actresses had the additional problem of leaf shreds sticking to their long skirts as they walked; by the end of the fourth act, the three sisters were covered in crunchy brown metaphors.

Faced with the options of undercutting his visual image for the show by getting rid of the leaves, or of jerking his actors around, the director did not hesitate. He took the cast through the play and eliminated big chunks of blocking they had spent weeks developing. Actors move onstage only when the psychological wants of their characters propel them to do so—at least that's the ideal for which good actors strive. But in this case a last-minute visual metaphor overruled the organic physicalization of the characters' emotional lives. The cast member to whom I spoke had argued with the director for keeping a particular cross that seemed especially important to him, and he was allowed to do so—"but I had to promise to do it lightly." The women in the show, because of the skirt problem, spent most of their time onstage standing still and talking.

Consider what these stories have in common: an overriding dependence on visual imagery that is not organic to the play at hand; halfhearted focus on the telling of the story; inattention to the artistic and practical needs of the actors; and meaningless compromises with the cast when challenged by them. Welcome to the director's theatre.

Contrast those stories with this one of a director's concept that worked. Eugene Ionesco's so-called anti-play *The Bald Soprano* is a romp of hilarious nonsequiturs and bizarre trivialities descending into chaos, all calculated to communicate the playwright's point that communication is impossible. In a production by the tiny non-Equity company Stage Actors Ensemble of Chicago, director James Clark had the actors perform with their eyes sealed shut with smooth, flesh-colored putty, as if all the characters had been born with no eyes or openings for them. He had rehearsed the actors blindfolded once the play was blocked and lines were memorized, drilling them until they could without sight execute their blocking and stage business, which included lighting cigarettes, dancing the tango, and pouring drinks.

The blindness of the characters was a perfect articulation of their inability to connect with one another. This was the whole idea of the concept, of course, but if it had been attempted merely with dark glasses and actors playing blind, it would have been a meaningless, unnecessary intrusion. The director's concept worked because the actors genuinely could not see but played their scenes as if they could: the play's point is that the characters don't realize they are cut off from one another. The concept also worked because it was embedded in what the actors had to do. It didn't exist behind them or around them, and it wasn't flown in over their heads. It didn't force the audience to choose between paying attention to the actors or watching the concept on parade. Instead of competing with the cast, it focused the audience's attention on the actors and let them embody the play. This is what good directing—no matter its specific style—always does.

The control problem plagues the relationship between the director and the actor more often than it does that between the director and the designer, for two reasons. The simpler one is that, at least in the United States, directors tend to be less than fully technically adept from a design standpoint. Most directors have done some acting, in many cases professionally, but it is a rare American director who used to be a designer. So directors here are more likely to welcome suggestions from designers than from actors.

The other reason has to do with the very nature of theatre. It is, once again, an actor's medium. The way to try to make it into a director's medium is to control the actor's work. The good director shapes and guides but does not try to control the actor's choices. The good director articulates the underlying psychological action of the character in terms apprehendable by the individual actor and coherent with the rest of the play. He or she then offers feedback and advice, as well as prodding and maybe even argument, as the actor proceeds to embody that psychological action in a series of moment-to-moment choices. The bad director controls the actor's work: dictates the choices. The only difference between the *auteur* director's fully realized production of a play and the puppet theatre production of the same play is the size of the payroll.

Your best service to the actor's medium is not to control but to enfranchise the actor as fully as possible. The fully enfranchised actor is the great strength of live theatre, really the only thing that can make live theatre memorable. An actor is enfranchised when brought to an understanding of the character so complete that it becomes visceral. Then that actor can simply live that character's life onstage every night.

This is that rare condition in which a piece of theatre becomes transcendent. Individual moments can be different from night to night without ever being false, because the actor truly inhabits the playwright's character. A false move has become an impossibility. The unenfranchised actor, on the other hand, lives outside the character and must therefore stick to reenacting the psychological choices that have been approved by the director. With no internal compass to keep the actor true, he or she cannot leave the path safely.

The point of the actor's art is not to become a star, of course. But certainly it is to connect with the audience, and only the enfranchised actor can do so. Joe Mantegna's performance in Gregory Mosher's production of *Glengarry Glen Ross* was unforgettable, as was that of Laurie Metcalf in John Malkovich's production of *Balm in Gilead*, and of Linda Stephens in Michael Maggio's production of the musical version of *Wings*. But who remembers who played either Portia or Shylock in Peter Sellars's nearly four-hour *Merchant of Venice*, or either Hamm or Clov in JoAnne Akalaitis's world-famous production of *Endgame*? The actors in question were in all likelihood first-rate, but who can see their work underneath all that directing?

When the actors in the actor's medium have been reduced to cogs in the director's machine, something is amiss.

Much in the culture of contemporary theatre promotes the disfranchising of the actor. Status in the theatre is hierarchical, with the director at the top and most actors near the bottom. This is not an inevitable structure but the result of decisions. It is also by no means a structure that is limited to shows directed by those who would be *auteurs*, but the structure is a part of the theatre's culture that enables the *auteur* theory to flourish.

Part of the problem is economic. We devalue what is plentiful, and there is nothing in the theatre more plentiful than actors. Because directors decide which actors get hired, directors are granted a status that proceeds not from the dynamic of earned authority but from its evil twin, the dynamic of power.

From the first point of contact between director and actor — usually the audition — the relationship is defined in terms of the director's power over the actor. In a typical situation the actors are kept waiting while the director sits in a room and has them brought in one at a time. Once inside the room, the actor may not exceed the time allotted for the audition, which is sometimes as short as ninety seconds, though the director may dismiss the actor without letting him or her use the full time. At the end of the audition, the actor is sent away without being told when — or if — he or she will hear another word about the job. Up to the moment the play is cast, there is no point at which the actors have been treated by the director as peers.

Once shaped this way by the casting process, the director/actor relationship holds true to form in rehearsals. How could it not? The actor's overriding professional consideration in this environment is inevitably to keep the director happy with the actor's work, which is not automatically the same thing as to be an artist.

Throw a clean ball against a dirty wall and it comes back dirty every time. The director who wishes to undermine the bad effects of the casting system must think about auditions differently. Bear in mind that in casting a play you are forming a community, and how you form it will define your own function in it.

Building the community begins at auditions, when you and the actors begin forming opinions about each other. This realization calls for a different approach to auditions. The most radical tools a director can bring to auditions are these: courtesy and consideration.

Insist that your producer set up specific appointments for precise times. This is generally how it works in auditions governed by Actors Equity rules, but outside of those situations anything can happen. Some theatres tell actors just to show up the day of the audition and then sign up for slots on a first-come, first-served basis. If it's a large audition, this guarantees that actors will spend up to several hours waiting to go in for their five-minute (if they're lucky) audition. Don't allow this to be done in your name.

As the actors are brought one by one into the room to audition, get off your chair and cross to them. Shake their hand, call them by name, and thank them for coming. Mean it. You are auditioning for them just as much as they are auditioning for you.

Chat for a moment. About them. You're the host here; be a gracious one. You have their resumé in front of you, and a quick glance at it will give you something to talk about. They've just been in a show you admired, or they've worked with a friend of yours, or it's apparent from their credits that they've just moved to town recently, or they claim fire-eating as a special skill, or something else on their resumé can trigger a few seconds of idle conversation. Break the ice.

If the audition is from the script to be produced, be prepared to sum up the play and the character from your point of view.

Don't eat or read during the audition. It seems like a burlesque of audition etiquette even to have to include this particular point, like Mark Twain's guide to correct behavior at funerals (one of his rules: "Do not bring your dog"), but a frequent complaint from actors is that directors feel free to polish off lunch or get absorbed in reading something during the actual audition. The actor is there for your benefit. Pay attention.

All this so far is not only minimally courteous, it also improves auditions. Putting people at ease brings out better work from them.

Let them finish. Let them finish. Let them finish. I have been at general auditions at a major regional theatre that employed a time-keeper with a stopwatch who would cut actors off if they ran long. This is an abominable practice, as is the well-known procedure of stopping an audition in process with a curt "Thank you" whenever the director happens to decide that the actor is unsuitable. It is more important that the people giving you their time at auditions be treated like adults than that the trains run on time. Make sure the appointments are scheduled so as to provide the actors with this fundamental civility, and then let them finish.

When they are done, get up again. Shake their hand again and thank them for coming. Then tell them something definite about notification. The most insulting thing about how actors are generally treated is that after their audition they are left hanging. If no call comes they eventually conclude they didn't get the job. It's the sort of lack of consideration that only power can get away with, that responsibility would never consider.

If you are seeing a good many people it may not be practical to notify everyone individually. But at least they can all be given a deadline by which time they can have a certainty. "Thanks for coming. Everyone who is called back will hear from us no later than Wednesday at five o'clock." If 5:01 Wednesday rolls around and they haven't heard, they know. It's better than leaving them hanging.

All these efforts should be undertaken not because it's good manners (though that is certainly reason enough) but because it will make your show better. It displays respect, and displays of respect are reciprocated. It begins to build a community wherein the actor understands that he or she is a valued colleague, not a useful underling. No other single understanding could energize your rehearsals more. Enfranchised actors understand that you are in rehearsals not to pass judgment on them but to help them go as far as they can.

Sometimes it's instructive to compare small things to great, so let us think about the task of directing rehearsals in light of the difference between Napoleon Bonaparte and George Washington.

Napoleon began his rise to dictator in the service of French democracy, quelling a Parisian revolt against the Republic, which led to his appointment as commander-in-chief, which led to his spectacular military victories in foreign lands, which led to his enormous popularity back home, which enabled him to seize dictatorial powers as first consul, which led to his crowning himself emperor. The possession of power generally incites the desire for more power, and Napoleon used the power that came his way the way most people would, for his own aggrandizement.

The other great general-turned-head-of-state of two hundred and some years ago used his power differently. Having led the victorious Revolution, and therefore finding himself in a position to convert his military prestige into political power, he instead resigned his commission and returned to private life. Coaxed out of retirement to become president as a near condition for ratifying the Constitution, he again stepped down when he thought staying would be counterproductive. He repeatedly transformed his power by surrendering it to the pursuit of an ethos, to something larger than himself. This is why Washington's republic continues to this day while Napoleon's empire exists only in history books.

So what does this have to do with directing *Harvey*?

Just this: the effective leader enfranchises the community to act for itself. He or she offers it a clear, coherent vision and makes sure the community has the tools to pursue that vision. Directors who shape their productions into personal statements are busy crowning themselves emperor. Effective directors surrender power to the pursuit of an ethos that will, if captured, transform their work into theatre that transcends their contribution to it.

The ethos to which you as director should surrender is this: the play never belongs to you. You are the deliveryman, and the play is the package. You have been entrusted with the package, but it is never yours.

Before an audience sees it, a play exists in one place only, as an imaginary four-dimensional moment in the mind of the playwright. When the playwright says of the play, "This is how I see it," he or she means that literally. Even the script is not the play in this sense; it is merely a description of the play, written out as the only practical way to share the real play—the imaginary play—with others. The production is not really the play either. It is, as Aristotle put it, "an imitation" of the real play, put together by a group of interpretive artists who have done their best to understand and articulate the description of the real play, which remains imaginary.

Come performance time, the play will finally exist in another place: the imagination of each audience member. The performance is over in the blink of an eye, but the play lingers: this is the point of all theatrical activity. Inevitably the play that each audience member receives will be somewhat different from those received by all the other audience members; but if you the director have done your job well, all those plays will nonetheless be fundamentally the playwright's play.

The director delivers the play from the playwright's imagination, as recorded in the script, to the actors, who will in turn deliver it to the audience. This delivery route is convoluted enough; even with the best of intentions, the package can easily get lost on the way. But if you do not strive to remain true to your best understanding of the play that the playwright imagined, the audience has no chance whatsoever of receiving that same play.

The ethos of the deliveryman alters the conventional director/

actor relationship by transforming *authority over* the actors into *responsibility to* them. Only the actors communicate directly with the audience, so you must give them what they need to do their job well, and then you must get out of their way. The countless directors who say they hate to let go of a show on opening night do not understand this.

At the beginning of the rehearsal period, the actors cannot be expected to be as intimate with the play as the director must be. And no two actors in the cast will have precisely identical—perhaps even compatible—impressions of the play at this point. Your responsibility to the cast is to make sure that the rehearsals proceed along a route of unified clarity. Articulate the playwright's intention to them; inspire and shape their contributions according to the needs of that intention.

In the course of production, your collaborators will bring to their jobs as designers and actors insights into the play that you hadn't seen. What used to be your best understanding of the play will now improve, and in turn you will have more to offer to your collaborators.

By the end of the rehearsal period, a talented cast that has been well directed will have a collective understanding of the play—and especially of their individual characters—that dwarfs anything the director might have to contribute at this point. But thanks to the director, the cast's play will still be the playwright's. As the ideal production opens, its actors have been enfranchised by the director to explore the play every night in ways that are true to the playwright's meaning and rooted in the playwright's vision. This exploration will discover things in the play that only those particular actors could find.

Once this is understood as the goal of directing a play, no conscientious director can knowingly use a production as a building block for mere Napoleonic self-expression.

3 : What Plays Are and How They Work

A *Streetcar Named Desire* tells the same story as *The Odd Couple*.

This is an illustrative thing to consider if you are concerned, as you must be, with understanding how plays work. There are more plays in the world than anyone can count. They can be taken apart and understood as a series of highly individual articulations of a very small number of stories.

Boy meets girl, boy loses girl, boy gets girl: that's a very popular story. The world's most popular story, of course, is about the obscure person who possesses hidden qualities that lift him or her to greatness. Its best-known version is the story of Cinderella, a story that itself has hundreds of versions, but it is also told onstage as *Abe Lincoln in Illinois* and *Saint Joan* and *The Miracle Worker* and *Evita*, among many others. It's also the story of Superman, of the Ugly Duckling, and of Jesus Christ. Yet another popular story is about the person who sets out on a journey or a quest and has interesting adventures along the way. This is the story of Huckleberry Finn, Odysseus, Dorothy Gale, Christian of *Pilgrim's Progress*, James Bond, and about a million others.

The story told by *Streetcar* and *Odd Couple* is not quite as primal as those stories, perhaps, but the fact that it is told by both the

Great American Drama and the Great American Comedy says something about our interest in hearing it.*

The story is this: There is a gruff, unrefined, overtly masculine slob who is the undisputed master of his home. There is a softer, more fastidious, more feminine, neurotic individual who is unhappily obsessed with a lost spouse. The slob suddenly finds himself saddled with the neurotic as a roommate. Through most of the play, he feels obliged to try to accommodate the situation as best he can. Finally he can't take it anymore and forcibly ejects his unwanted roommate. Both plays end with the resumption of poker-playing.

Tennessee Williams's version of the story is about a human being's relationship with Fate, which is to say it is tragic. Neil Simon's is about how two human beings relate to each other, which is to say it is comic. And so they have the different resolutions appropriate to each: Blanche is shattered, Oscar and Felix are improved as people. But they are versions of the same story nonetheless.

Is this a useful observation, or is it more of a party trick? Well, the solitary half of the director's job consists of sitting alone and reading the play over and over again, and thinking about the play, and researching the play, and reading it some more, and coming to decisions about what happens in the play and what that action means. The object of all this cloistered endeavor is to understand the play in its essential form.

Toward this end, the ability to analyze a script in order to understand its dramatic action is a vital skill to acquire. The most sensible guide to analyzing plays ever written is *The Poetics* by Aristotle. Some of it is boring, some of it is irrelevant, some of it depends upon knowledge of ancient Greek texts that are lost, some small parts of it are even offensive. Despite all that, it remains, twenty-three centuries after it was written, a clear explanation of what plays do and how they do it. In fact, the best thing you could do for your-

---

*As far as I know, Richard Christiansen of the *Chicago Tribune* was the first to call *The Odd Couple* "the great American comedy" in print, and I have cheerfully lifted the designation from him.

self right now would be to fling this book aside and go buy a copy of *The Poetics.*

Aristotle's book is immortal and priceless because in it he gives a surpassingly functional definition of tragedy, and then lists and explains the six elements he finds in each and every play. Three of them are especially important to the task of analyzing a play.

(Parenthetically, by *tragedy* the Greeks meant simply a serious play on serious themes, essentially what we mean when we say *drama*—except that the Greeks expected all plays to include music, whereas for us that's optional. Some Greek tragedies have happy endings; one or two of them we might even call romances if they were written today. The Greeks called them all tragedies. If, say, *Inherit the Wind, The Birthday Party*, or *Carousel* had been around in ancient Athens, the Greeks would have called them tragedies too.)

So. Aristotle's definition of tragedy. This is from the second paragraph of Part Six of *The Poetics* (in the translation by S. H. Butcher):

> Tragedy, then, is an imitation of an action that is serious, complete, and of a certain magnitude; in language embellished with each kind of artistic ornament, the several kinds being found in separate parts of the play; in the form of action, not of narrative; through pity and fear effecting the purgation of these emotions.

Let's sort through this. Look again at the first part: "an imitation of an action that is serious, complete, and of a certain magnitude." What exactly does it mean?

It means three things. First, to be considered a serious play on serious themes—a tragedy—the play can't be just silly. *Hellzapoppin'* doesn't qualify here. Second, it can't tell only part of a story. If the action is Lear railing against the storm, this will be meaningless to an audience unless they are shown how he got there, that he has entrusted his well-being to people who do not love him; also, the audience will be left unsatisfied unless they are allowed to see what happens to this great, foolish man, that his rage on the heath leads him to peace. Finally, the play must be about something important enough to warrant an audience's attention. A play about me achieving self-knowledge might well be tragic, but one about me eating breakfast is not.

The second part: "in language embellished with each kind of artistic ornament, the several kinds being found in separate parts of the play." Later Aristotle says that by this he means "language into which rhythm, 'harmony,' and song enter." For our purposes, what's important here is that the language in a play is shaped and heightened, compared to language in real life. There's a lot of randomness in normal everyday conversation, and no good playwright will simply transcribe that. He or she will select and mold the language to achieve whatever the specific artistic aim might be.

The next part is vital: "in the form of action, not of narrative." "Action" is the only noun Aristotle uses twice in the definition. It deserves the emphasis. A play is not a short story or an essay. It is an imitation of an action: it doesn't tell us what the characters think, it shows us what they do. All characters in all plays do whatever they do because they want something from the other characters with whom they interact. Their actions are attempts to fulfill their wants. Even if a playwright gives us a character who narrates, that narration is part of a throughline of action. The Stage Manager in *Our Town* narrates as part of an ongoing relationship with the audience, from whom he wants something. Telling us what he tells us is an attempt to get it. That's active, and that's what a play must be.

Finally: "through pity and fear effecting the purgation of these emotions." Elsewhere in *The Poetics* Aristotle calls this emotional response "the true tragic pleasure."

We get satisfaction from watching a serious play to the degree that the play calls up pity and fear in us and then purges them. We get no healthy pleasure from wallowing in pity and fear but rather from working through them and getting them out of our systems.

It's not that we're happy that Blanche DuBois gets raped, or that Willy Loman dies a failure, or that the Elephant Man has a horribly disfiguring disease. But the plays that tell these stories are deeply satisfying to us because they evoke pity and fear by reminding us of the fragile nature of all human existence. We feel compassion for these protagonists because we would prefer to think that people like us don't deserve such terrible fates. And on some inner level we fear for ourselves, not because we think these precise situations will happen to us but because seeing these characters in these precise situations reminds us once again that we have no assurance of anything.

> Every Tragedy, therefore, must have six parts, which parts determine its quality—namely, Plot, Character, Diction, Thought, Spectacle, Song.
>
> —*Poetics*, Part Six

The simplest form of the drama may well be the anecdotal joke. Jokes are always put in the present tense, as are stage directions, to feed the illusion that the story being told is happening right now:

> A guy goes into a bar with a duck on his head. Bartender says, "Where'dja get the jackass?" Guy says, "That's no jackass, it's a duck." Bartender says, "I was talkin' to the duck."

This lovely joke—which consists entirely of a stage direction and three lines of dialogue—is completely vacant of any of the details we might include if we wished to convey a sense of character.

Is the man young or old? Is he married? Is the bartender a ruddy-faced Irishman with a brogue you could cut with a knife, or a tattooed ex-sailor from Maine? Why does the man have a duck on his head? Does the bartender consider him a jackass *because* he has a duck on his head, or is there some previous history between the two that inclines him to that opinion? Is the man, in fact, a jackass or not? And the duck: is it a mallard or a bufflehead? Has it been trained to sit on the man's head, or did it do so of its own volition? Is it nesting there, or has it stopped off briefly on its way south? And when the bartender asks the duck his question, does he honestly expect it to answer?

We don't care about any of these questions, and we are right not to do so. The joke—the three-line play—asks us only to care about the plot. Questions of characterization are irrelevant. Successful jokes relate a specific funny event clearly. Jokes that sacrifice the comedic structure of set-up followed by punchline, in order to describe the characters, tend not to hold their listeners.

In plays, as in jokes, plot is more important than character. A play is an imitation of an action, not of a person. Obviously, action doesn't occur without a person acting, but it is the action, not the person, that is important. This is what Aristotle means when he calls plot "the soul of the tragedy" and says, "Without action there cannot be a tragedy; there may be without character."

Key to understanding plot is his defining it as "the *arrangement* of the incidents." By themselves, a bunch of interesting incidents do not a plot make. A plot is a structure: the plot is how the playwright assembles the incidents.

For example, the two incidents in the story of Oedipus that everyone knows are that he murdered his father and married his mother. But these two events are not actually even *in* the play *Oedipus the King.* The genius of Sophocles' plot is that his play takes place years after those incidents have occurred, on the day that Oedipus discovers he has done these horrible things. Instead of a plot that meanders over the course of many years, we are given the tightly compacted events of a single day. The murder and the incest are made vivid to us in the freshness of Oedipus's discovery of them. The plot focuses our attention where it should be: on Oedipus's struggle for self-knowledge, not on his crimes. We don't give a hoot about Oedipus's father, after all; we care about Oedipus's learning that he killed him. The structure, the plot, the way Sophocles chooses to tell the story makes us care about the one and not the other.

Another example: The events of Harold Pinter's *Betrayal* are mundane. A woman has an affair that goes on for years with her husband's best friend. We see the three of them in various combinations over the years as the affair begins, continues, and ends. The power of the play comes from its backward-moving plot. Pinter has arranged the incidents in reverse chronological order, so the play begins with a dead relationship on display and finishes with the first flirtations of two people attracted to each other. At every point in the play except the very beginning, we the audience know what the characters cannot know: what will happen to them next. We know that the flirtations will turn into lies and that love will grow hollow. The plot—the arrangement of the incidents—has charged every moment of the love story with death: the soul of the tragedy indeed.

Second in importance in every tragedy is character, which Aristotle defines as "habitual action." You are what you do.

He also describes character as "that which reveals moral purpose, showing what kind of things a man chooses or avoids."

Blanche DuBois's habitual action is to seek a safe haven. It is the only thing she does in the entire play. She does it repeatedly, in continually varying forms. She comes to New Orleans in the first place because she knows her sister Stella will take care of her. She tries to get Mitch to marry her, and she tries to get Shep Huntleigh on the phone, because she thinks each of them will rescue her. She drinks too much, for the sake of the temporary haven it provides from reality, just as she has been sexually promiscuous because doing so created the temporary haven of the illusion of being loved. At the end of the play, after her sanity has been broken, she fights off those who have come to take her to an institution, until the doctor talks to her softly and persuades her that he represents a safe haven for her, and then she goes willingly.

At each point in the play at which she can avoid one thing and choose another, she avoids the challenge of independence and chooses the hope that she can put herself into someone else's hands and be safe. The one full scene in the play in which she has no such choice available to her is the one full scene in which she is alone with Stanley, and it is in this scene that she is destroyed.

Her need to seek a safe haven, this need that so completely defines her, is sometimes called in modern theatre her throughline, or her spine, or her superobjective. Aristotle is simpler. He calls it her character. It is who she is.

The third most important item on the list of ingredients of a tragedy is Thought. Aristotle says that by Thought in a play he means "the faculty of saying what is possible and pertinent in given circumstances." *What happens in the play?* is the question of Plot. Thought—essentially what we might call Theme—asks a different question: *What does the play mean?*

A popular but misleading way to think of theme is as the moral of the story, as in Aesop's fables: The Lesson to Be Learned. Theme in a play is not like a theme in an essay, it's more like a theme in music. The theme of an essay is the explicit point with which the writer hopes the reader or listener will be brought to agree. "That government is best which governs least." "Yes, Virginia, there is a Santa Claus." "From *every* mountainside, let freedom ring."

A theme in music is different. "Da da da dum" is Beethoven's most famous theme, and I'm not sure he is trying to enlist our intellectual agreement with it. He states it and restates it, articulating it first this way and then that, building a rich, magnificent symphony around these four notes.

What does the Fifth Symphony mean?

Nothing, and everything. The question could be answered differently by each listener, and each answer would be valid. The same is true of a play: *Hamlet* has been produced in tens of thousands of theatres over the course of four hundred years, and will continue to be so for centuries to come because each production finds its own specific meaning in the play. Art is a relationship with an audience, and that audience contributes meaning to the event. Even the artist who is in total control of his or her artwork is not in control of what that artwork means to an audience. So the question of theme in a play is a murky one.

David Mamet says that plays work on subconscious themes, the way dreams do. Dreaming is our subconscious mind's way of working out problems that for one reason or other elude our conscious mind. We dream in metaphors that our subconscious mind can explore as it looks for a solution to the literal problem that stumps us during the day. Likewise with plays: by depicting the actions of characters in a situation of crisis, a play deals with thematic issues that are not susceptible to conscious exploration. A good play doesn't make statements, it asks questions to which it seeks answers. The dream-metaphor that is the play is put onstage, and it interacts with the audience's subconscious dream-lives; the play is successful if its subtextual theme speaks to the audience's subconscious confusion.

In other words, the theme of *Oedipus the King* cannot be this: "It is a poor idea to murder one's father and marry one's mother." Our conscious minds can easily grasp this notion, so it would be a banal topic for drama. Nor can it be "Count no man happy until he is dead," which is the gist of the Chorus's last speech. This idea is certainly part of the play, but our conscious minds have no trouble grasping it either, so it is not likely to be the idea in the play that animates our dream-lives. Sophocles' play is profoundly meaningful exactly because its theme runs deep into our subconscious minds.

So what is that theme? Your answer to that might well be different from my answer, but here's mine. The theme—the main question in our hearts to which the play speaks subtextually—is this: "Am I a good person?"

The question is asking whether the normal range of human frailty and moral failure is really our fault or not. Oedipus did not intend to commit patricide and incest. Upon learning of a prophecy that he would do these things, he fled the country where the couple who raised him lived, the couple whom he believed to be his parents. He came to Thebes, where his actual parents lived unknown to him, and unwittingly carried out the prophecy. His guilt is unmerited, yet his guilt is an objective fact. He did his best to avoid killing his father and marrying his mother, yet he really did both those things. Is he a good person?

It is exactly the theme raised by the Christian doctrine of original sin, which goes to show how universal a question it is. Christianity teaches that we are all born carrying the guilt of Adam and Eve's disobedience in Eden, and the purpose of baptism is to wash our souls clean of this blot. The original sin is not something any of us did, but we inherit its stain simply by virtue of being human. The church says to its adherents what fate says to Oedipus: "Your guilt in this matter is unmerited, yet your guilt is an objective fact."

Are we in every way the person we believe ourselves to be? If not, will we someday be punished for that self-deception? Is our very nature something we should try to avoid? Does the simple fact of being human mean we should seek redemption?

These questions aren't created by the play, they are merely raised by it. The questions already exist in our hearts before we walk into the theatre. Most important, these questions are not open to empirical answers. They need to be answered individually by each of us. This is why they work as themes for a play. *Oedipus* has been in production for two and a half millennia because the fundamental question it asks resonates deeply with the themes of our collective subconscious.

Plot, Character, and Thought: these are the elements of a play upon which you must reflect as you come to decisions about the play. What happens in the play, what underlying psychological action do the events of the play boil down to, and what is the broader meaning of that action?

The other three elements on Aristotle's list—Diction, for which read the skill of the actors you will cast; Song; and Spectacle, for which read design elements and the physical staging of the piece— will come into play later, when you implement the decisions that you make at this early stage.

As you think about and plan for the play you will direct, seize this fact: a play consists of action, and of action only. The plot is composed of action; each character is nothing but a set of actions so consistent with one another that they can be considered habitual; and the theme emerges for each audience member through the interaction of character and plot.

This is just as well, after all, because action is what a director directs.

4 : Action and Metaphor

An actor was rehearsing for a London production of John Logan's *Never the Sinner*. "I see this scene," his director told him at one difficult point, "in terms of the way the sunlight looks when it comes through the windows at Westminster Abbey."

"Fine," the actor replied. "What do you want me to *do?*"

Plays are interesting to watch because they are both action and metaphor: a play depicts a dramatic action that is a metaphor for real life. As director, you must understand the play in two different ways, and each way requires that you answer a different question.

What happens in the play? addresses the play as action, and can be answered fairly objectively, though at different levels of perceptiveness. *Vladimir and Estragon wait for Godot* is accurate as far as it goes, but it is less perceptive than *Vladimir and Estragon devise ways to pass the time while waiting for Godot*, which is in its turn less perceptive than *Vladimir and Estragon devise ways to pass the time while Vladimir waits for Godot and Estragon clings to Vladimir.*

The second question, *What does this action mean?*, addresses the play as metaphor, and valid answers will be as diverse as any range of thoughtful opinions about any work of art. One director may see *Waiting for Godot* as a statement of the hopelessness of human existence. Another may see it as a testament to the power of faith, the belief in things unseen. It is impossible to say that either, or any other thoughtful, interpretation is incorrect. This is one reason it's a great play.

The artists that come together to put on a play have divergent areas of specialty. Actors specialize in doing things. Hence the name. The way for a director to be helpful to an actor is to talk in verbs: *conceal, persuade, protect, seduce, resist, destroy, expose,* and so on. What the actor needs to know is what the character is trying to do from moment to moment. The answer is always a verb.

The descriptive power of metaphor, by contrast, is essentially static and therefore not of great use to an actor. Understanding why Arthur Miller called his play *The Crucible* will not tend to help most actors in it play their scenes better.

Designers, on the other hand, specialize in metaphor.

A set design is more than just an environment for the action. The physical world of a play is a metaphor for its theme.

Godot's road through a nearly barren landscape is a metaphor for the essence of the world in which its protagonists live. A country road and a tree: an apparently unending journey and a single landmark are all that seem to exist for Vladimir and Estragon, who go on forever but are always at the same point. At the beginning of the second act, the tree has sprouted a handful of leaves. "Not to show hope or inspiration," Beckett told Roger Blin, the play's first director, "but only to record the passage of time."

Eugene Lee's set design for the Broadway production of Stephen Sondheim and Hugh Wheeler's *Sweeney Todd: The Demon Barber of Fleet Street* depicted Victorian London in a way that emphasized the exploitation and dehumanization that is central to the show's theme. At the top of the show, a frontdrop displays a giant illustration of the class system entitled "The British Beehive." This is torn down as a factory whistle blows, revealing an almost characterless network of industrial-looking platforms, stair units, and catwalks that will need to be wheeled around the stage by members of the chorus as the play progresses, against a monochromatic backdrop of factories and tenements. Amidst this harshness live the murderers, victims, beggars, corrupt officials, frauds, imprisoned lunatics, and unwitting cannibals who populate the musical.

The absence of conventional scenery that Thornton Wilder requires for *Our Town* is part and parcel of that play's heart and soul. As the play unfolds, the actors set up a few chairs or a couple of stepladders on a bare stage to represent whatever scenery they need. This theatrical minimalism enlists the audience's imagination in the creation of the world of the play. Wilder shows us that we can find beauty and magic in the informed manipulation of homely objects; this production technique mirrors the play's comprehensive idea— "so simple that it is momentous," John Gassner wrote of it—that everyday life is a thing of wonder.

Costume designs are metaphors for the characters. You are what you wear. This is why it is psychologically right that Lois Lane and Jimmy Olson don't recognize Clark Kent as Superman. It is also why productions of *Hamlet* that wish to emphasize Hamlet's melancholy nature costume him in black, and it is why, to help convey the suggestion of a moth in Blanche DuBois's manner, Tennessee Williams specifies that her costume be white.

In the original Broadway production of John Kander and Fred Ebb's *Cabaret*, the Master of Ceremonies was conceived as an exotic Other, and his costume reflected that. With his black tie and tails, slicked-down hair, whitened face, and lipstick, he seemed to audiences in the 1960s to have stepped in from another world. And so he had: his cabaret was Berlin in the '30s, represented onstage through a fourth-wall convention. The audience watched from regular theatre seats; a distorting mirror backdrop during the cabaret scenes put their image onstage, but warped it first so that it wasn't really them.

But the 1990s Broadway revival of the show had something else to say about the Master of Ceremonies, so it revamped the character by changing his clothes. In this production he is no longer an Other. His clothes are not formal; adorned by visible track marks on his arms and a swastika tattoo on one buttock, sometimes he wears not much at all. It's clearly a theatrical design, but a less showbizzy version of him could blend in among the netherworld denizens of any contemporary American big city. He is stylized, but he is One of Us, which befits a production at which the audience sits not in conventional theatre seating but at nightclub tables, so that it is always part of—not just spectators to—his cabaret.

Lighting design differs from set and costume design in that it exists in time as well as in the three physical dimensions. It is a metaphor for the action itself.

Sometimes this metaphor is overt, as in William Gibson's *The Miracle Worker*. Each of that play's three acts begins in darkness: Act One in the dead of the night that the infant Helen Keller is made blind and deaf by fever; Act Two in the evening, as Annie Sullivan struggles with how she might approach the challenges of trying to teach Helen (when the morning comes in this act, it begins with a single shaft of sunlight hitting the outdoor water pump, while Annie, inside, says, ". . . Obedience is the gateway through which knowledge enters the mind of the child"); and Act Three in the predawn of the day Helen makes her great breakthrough.

For almost all of the play, sunlight is either absent or dying. The only scene before Act Three that takes place in the morning is the one in which Annie makes her first big step forward in teaching Helen, by getting her to eat with silverware from her own plate. For the most part, to the degree that it is possible onstage and still have the audience see the action, Helen lives in a world without light.

The metaphor pays off in Act Three. It is evening, and the light is again fading toward darkness as the Keller family is unwittingly undoing Annie's work by indulging Helen's wildness at supper. Annie has taken Helen to the water pump in the twilit yard to make her refill the water pitcher she deliberately spilled.

"And then," the stage direction says, "the miracle happens . . . there is a change in the sundown light, and with it a change in Helen's face, some light coming into it that we have never seen there. . . ." A moment later, with Helen having received the gift of language, Gibson specifies that dusk has continued to grow, "except over the pump," where Annie and Helen are. As the play ends, and they cross the yard to the house, the light spreads and brightens.

Sometimes the metaphor is less overt. A century ago A. C.

Bradley pointed out in his published lectures Shakespeare's metaphoric use of light in *Macbeth*, and I cannot do better than to summarize his observations as follows.

Darkness and the oppressive murkiness of night are the main symbols, apart from the imagery of blood, that inform the action of the tragedy. The impression *Macbeth* leaves is, in Bradley's words, "the impression of a black night broken by flashes of light and color." Nearly all the scenes of the play that stick in the memory occur in darkness, from Macbeth's seeing a dagger before him to the murders of Duncan and Banquo to Lady Macbeth's sleepwalking; Macbeth's visits to the "black and midnight hags" are set in a cavern.

When light appears, it is for the most part vivid and horrifying: the thunderstorm of the first scene, the torch that lights Banquo's route to his death and that is obliterated by one of his murderers, the fire under the witches' cauldron that emits light from below as if it were hellfire, the candlelight that reveals Lady Macbeth's wasted face. Natural sunlight seems to occur only once in the play after Duncan's murder, and that is near its close, when Malcolm's army has gathered to unseat and destroy Macbeth.

Shakespeare's use of the metaphor, especially remarkable as he wrote for a theatre that lacked controllable stage lights, is elegant. Like the sunlight itself, the natural political order that Macbeth has perverted and debased can only reassert itself when he is to be eliminated.

When you discuss the play in conferences with your designers, metaphor will at some point be a necessary topic. This doesn't mean that you as director must devise metaphors for each aspect of the show. They are the ones who specialize in it, after all. If it's really the case that you see, say, Juliet's nurse as an eggplant, or the War of the Roses as the whirling apart of Yugoslavia, by all means make that clear to your designers so that they don't have to guess where you are trying to take the show.

But you might be better off talking to them about the play itself, and letting them respond in metaphor to your clarity about the play's action, characters, and theme. Jeff Bauer's set design for Court Theatre's A *Delicate Balance* was a room that seemed to float precariously in space, disconnected from any outside reality. One could look at the set and know what the play was about. All the director had said to Bauer was the prosaic fact that Tobias's house was a place where people came to escape from their problems.

So if there's a scene in the play you're directing that reminds you of the sunlight in Westminster Abbey, be sure to discuss the point in detail with your lighting designer. But do your actors a big favor and leave them alone about it.

5 : Telling the Actors Where to Stand

A DIRECTOR MAKES a play make sense by staging its action, so the problem of directors distorting plays is partially reducible to a wrong approach to the question of staging.

In a production of Sophocles' *Electra*, a director at an important regional theatre had a pool of water built into the set. In the play's final moments, confronted by Electra and Orestes intent on his death, Aegisthus dove into the pool and vanished.

In the absence of any dialogue referring to this event, the audience was left wondering. Did Aegisthus commit suicide by drowning rather than be killed by his enemies? Or did he escape? Perhaps he drowned trying to escape? A conclusion not available to the audience was the one Sophocles scripted: that Orestes takes Aegisthus inside the house and kills him.

An acclaimed Broadway revival of Eugene O'Neill's *Long Day's Journey into Night* distorted that play's final moment more subtly. In the course of her final monologue, wherein she believes she is back in her senior year at convent school discussing her future with Mother Elizabeth, Mary Tyrone's roamings around the room brought her to stand directly behind her husband James, who was seated down center facing the audience. She placed her hands on his shoulders as she tried to remember what it was that kept her from becoming a nun, then spoke the play's last words: "Yes, I remember. I fell in love with James Tyrone and was so happy for a time." James, in obvious agony, reached up to her in a gesture of supplication and support as the lights faded to black.

Placing James Tyrone down center, sitting in a chair facing the audience, keeps focus on him during Mary's final monologue, so that her speech is no more important than his unspoken reaction to it. Bringing her to stand behind him for her final words, and especially having her place her hands on his shoulders, inevitably made her seem aware of his presence and perhaps even speaking these last sentences for his benefit. Again, it made him as focal in the moment as she. In the next moment he became more so, as he reached for her. The production's final image was not of Mary's pain but of James's compassion for her pain.

This presentation is at odds with what the playwright has written. O'Neill has provided extensive stage directions—as much a part of the play as any of the lines—that make the following clear: James is sitting at the dining table with Jamie and Edmund, in a "hopeless stupor" from the whiskey he has been drinking with his sons. It is Mary who sits facing the audience during her last speech, on the sofa, apart from the men and clearly unaware of them. O'Neill repeatedly indicates that she stares "before her"—that is to say, toward us and away from her family. When she finishes speaking, James communicates no response of any sort. O'Neill says merely that he "stirs in his chair" while their sons "remain motionless" and Mary "stares before her in a sad dream." In O'Neill's final moment, Mary is alone in every sense of the word.

Let us assume what cannot always be assumed, that in *Electra* and in *Long Day's Journey* each director's goal was to communicate the playwright's meaning. Something less precise was communicated instead. The meaning of each play was muddied.

Why did Aegisthus dive into the water? If it was intended as a symbolic rendering of his death at the hand of Orestes, the effect was merely bewildering. If it was to be taken literally as either escape or suicide, which was it, and why was it unremarked upon by any of the characters who witnessed it?

And if James Tyrone is so all-fired compassionate, why exactly does his family resent him so?

The problem is this: staging choices convey meanings. Staging choices that are at odds with those of the playwright but are inserted into the overall context of the play will confuse the careful viewer.

Follow the thought process through an imaginary example of a mistaken directing choice. It is the final scene of your production of Arthur Miller's *Death of a Salesman*. Here's what is scripted: Willy Loman is dead and buried. Charley, Biff, and Happy have argued over the meaning of Willy's life and death, and have left the gravesite. Linda has remained to say goodbye to Willy. Her speech begins with: "Forgive me, dear. I can't cry." She goes on to say that she can't understand why Willy committed suicide, and concludes: "I made the last payment on the house today. Today, dear. And there'll be nobody home. We're free and clear. We're free. We're free. We're free." Biff comes over and helps her to her feet, and she does cry as they exit together.

But let's say that during rehearsals you come up with the bold stroke of having Linda remove her wedding ring (perhaps as she says the words "there'll be nobody home") and drop it, without affection, into the dirt of Willy's grave. This gives the scene an undeniable theatrical charge, it raises the stakes of the speech incredibly high, it adds a new level of meaning to "We're free," and it makes Willy's failure devastatingly complete. It also adds a complex aspect to Linda's character that makes us realize that her story is not over and wonder what she will do next. Or so you tell yourself.

Further, you persuade yourself, it doesn't contradict anything in the script. Not a word of Linda's speech would need to be altered in any way to accommodate the new business. Although Miller might not have thought of it, the impulse behind Linda rejecting her ring is implicit in the tension of the moment anyway. If that weren't so, after all, the idea wouldn't have come to you in the first place. Again: or so you tell yourself.

When the scene is played before an audience, those seeing the play for the first time have no way of knowing that the Linda Loman that Miller wrote—the one who, at the end of the play, doesn't understand what her husband did but loves him anyway—has been replaced by you with a different Linda, one who rejects his memory. Some who are familiar with the play may, without giving the matter much thought, approve of the innovation as a fresh take on the material or an updating of the character. You may well run little risk of encountering disapproval.

The depressing thing about this imaginary choice is that, bad as it is, it is not much of a parody. It is not noticeably less plausible than the real-life bad choices already mentioned. The audience member who has picked up on what Miller has written into Linda's character as well as what you have directed into it will be unable either to separate or reconcile the two, and will have a vague sense that Miller has not been clear. Just as at the productions of *Electra* and *Long Day's Journey* mentioned earlier, the thoughtful audience member in this imaginary example is left confused.

The sort of bad directing I describe here is widespread because it is easier to do than good directing.

Good directing requires that you subordinate yourself to the play in a way that transcends mere familiarity with it. "When I was able to feel things rightly, the play came to life," Stanislavski wrote about his first work as a director. "Where there was only outward ingenuity, the play remained a dead thing." The inner life of a play is reachable only through constant questioning of one's own assumptions, constant examination of what the playwright actually wrote, constant digging, constant simplification, constant learning about the life of another's mind. This, to say the least, is hard. No director can do this job perfectly well 100 percent of the time.

You can intermittently escape this hard job, or even avoid it entirely, by taking on the much easier job of substituting craft for art. The specific craft that's helpful in this way is a director's cultivated knack for visual images and stage pictures. This knack is an absolute necessity for a director to develop, but it can cut two ways. In a production wherein things are felt rightly, a mastery of visual craft can make the difference between a solid production and a breathtaking one. But in lesser productions, or even lesser moments within good productions, a director's eye for pictures and imagery can obscure the inability or unwillingness to commit to the underlying psychological action of the play. The poignancy of the married Tyrones longing together for their vanished happiness makes a lovely stage picture. An actor disappearing into a pool of water is such an unusual sight onstage that it automatically commands attention. Our imaginary staging of Linda Loman's final speech could give the moment a tough, uncompromising jolt. It is, all in all, not that hard for a director with talent or experience to devise stage moments that are interesting to watch.

Your job as a director is to present the play as a unity, to bring the various elements of the production into one clear focus that expresses your best judgment of the playwright's intentions. The ideal production of a play hangs like a mobile from a single thread.

Because theatre is collaborative, much of a director's contribution has to do with shaping the contributions of others. The better you do this part of the job, the less visible will be your hand in it, and the less credit you will receive as your actors and designers win praise. This is as it should be.

Staging is the one ingredient in a production that is recognizable to the onlooker as clearly the director's contribution. A director who wishes to be considered an *auteur* will therefore elevate the importance of staging to the production, which as we have seen can pull the play out of unity.

Aristotle tells us that Spectacle is the least of the elements of tragedy. "The Spectacle has, indeed, an emotional attraction of its own, but, of all the parts, it is the least artistic, and . . . depends more on the art of the stage machinist than on that of the poet."

Spectacle consists of the craft of providing visual interest in the presentation of the play. It can be provided by the playwright, the designer, the director, or the actor. When Tennessee Williams has Laura Wingfield blow out her candles, he is recognizing the value of Spectacle. So were Gregory Mosher and Michael Merritt when they decided that the plays-within-the-play scenes of David Mamet's *A Life in the Theatre* should be played to the back wall of the stage, so the audience watches as if from backstage (a director/designer choice that Mamet now suggests in the published script). Eugene

Ionesco wrote Berenger's transformation in *Rhinoceros* to occur off-stage, so the actor could put on green makeup and a horn. Zero Mostel, playing the role, insisted that the only way to transform into a rhinoceros was to do so onstage, in full view of the audience, using no special makeup or costume pieces but only the skill of the actor. Ionesco doubted that such a piece of Spectacle was possible until he saw Mostel do it.

These pieces of Spectacle all work because each helps to make sense of the play. None exploits the play for its own sake. But Spectacle can become the main occupation of the director, and when that happens the cart is before the horse.

Craft not in the service of art is empty. Staging that does not express the inner life of the playwright's play, no matter its surface brilliance, fails because it serves only itself. The answer to the question *Why did Aegisthus dive into the water?* is this: "Because the director thought it looked cool." This is a form of sloppiness.

An undisciplined approach to art requires sloppiness in craft. If you don't do the hard job of subordinating yourself to the play's inner life, you will fall back on the easier job of displaying outward ingenuity. But the application of craft that is ungrounded in the truth of the art is necessarily a scattershot affair.

Empty staging corrupts the play's meaning, which then further corrupts staging. The cycle continues until the meaning of the play and the meaning of the production part company entirely. If James Tyrone is made compassionate by the staging of the final scene, that choice will need to be justified by choices throughout the rest of the play. Indeed, in the Broadway production that made this choice, Tyrone came across as a gruff but caring patriarch who was underappreciated by his family. The complicated character that O'Neill wrote never made it onto the stage.

If you get away with taking the easy way out too often, eventually you will come to mistake it for your real job. Your artistic skills will decay without your even knowing it, as you hone your debased (because empty) craft. You will become more and more skilled at staging moments which you then string together, and less and less able to direct a play.

The solution is to make sure that the scene's content chooses the staging, not the other way around. Staging is a conveyance for meaning. It is the grammar with which the director speaks, not the subject he or she addresses. The director's challenge is to ensure that the meaning conveyed by the staging is the playwright's.

This has nothing to do with mindlessly following the printed stage directions, or with mounting museum reproductions of the way the play was produced originally.

It has everything to do with understanding that to direct a play is to tell a story. Tell the story you were given. Pay attention to stage directions that were actually written by the playwright. Many directors pride themselves on not even reading a published script's printed stage directions. This is because they know that an acting edition of a play frequently contains stage directions that the playwright didn't write, that are merely a stage manager's record of the blocking and stage business that was used in the New York production. They are right to prefer to devise their own work in these matters. But they forget, or choose to ignore, that the script also contains stage directions that the playwright *did* write. They are easy to distinguish from the other stage directions because they are about things that matter, and they should be read by the director. If you are directing *A Raisin in the Sun*, you need to know that Walter Lee is purposely hurting his mother by telling her repeatedly that he has been skipping work to go to the Green Hat bar to drink. *Each time he says "Green Hat" he is quietly twisting the knife in Mama* is how Lorraine Hansberry puts it in the script. On the other hand, the script also provides information you don't need to know: that just before this speech, as staged on Broadway, the actor playing Walter sat on the downstage arm of the chair downstage right. But you can't sort out these two pieces of information unless you read both.*

---

*I know of a director, who is surely not unique in this regard, who routinely blacks out all the stage directions in a script before she distributes copies to the actors. She does this with unproduced and unpublished plays wherein the stage directions could only be the playwright's, as well as with established scripts which are likely to include stage directions by others. She was once directing a reading—not a production, not even a workshop, but a reading—of a play by an

If you change any of the playwright's stage directions, make sure that in doing so you don't change the arc of the character or the focus of the moment. Mostel's insistence on ignoring the scripted exit for the rhinoceros transformation was true to the character and the moment, as Ionesco himself acknowledged. The director of *Electra* who has Aegisthus dive into the pool has changed the character and the moment beyond recognition.

If these points sound elementary, it's because they are. Basic though they may be, to follow them rigorously would require a fundamental departure from the school of directing now in vogue. A director could observe all these points and still direct poorly, of course. But no director could observe these points conscientiously and turn out any of the misbegotten stagings discussed in this chapter. The decadence of much of contemporary directing proceeds from the director's art becoming severed from the director's craft. Some improvement in the situation can be accomplished by addressing the craft end of the problem.

out-of-town playwright. They were five days into their week of rehearsals (a full week of rehearsals for a reading: always a bad sign) when the playwright got a phone call from the director. She was stumped. The actors and she couldn't figure out why the character Hildegard suddenly fell silent in the final moments of the play. Two pages before the end, Hildegard just stopped having lines, but there was no apparent reason for her to have exited. Why was she silent? With a certain amount of understandable satisfaction, the playwright read the director the pertinent stage direction: "Aurora fires the gun, four shots, into Hildegard."

6 : The Show That Needs a Dramaturg Has a Bad Director

A GENERATION OR SO AGO, the dramaturg had virtually no place in the American theatre. Nowadays it seems you can't swing a dead cat without hitting one. The dramaturg's emergence has been contemporaneous with—and, I submit, caused by—the growing decadence of the director's art.

Dramaturgy is an unappealing word but a vital idea. Its general definition encompasses almost the whole of theatrical activity, but in the context of what dramaturgs do, dramaturgy is a comprehensive exploration of the contexts in which the play resides. The dramaturg is the resident expert on the physical, social, political, and economic milieus in which the action takes place, the psychological underpinnings of the characters, the various metaphorical expressions in the play of thematic concerns; as well as on technical consideration of the play as a piece of writing: structure, rhythm, flow, even individual word choices.

There are different sorts of dramaturgs, with varying responsibilities, though few dramaturgs are of a pure type; most overlap categories. The institutional dramaturg helps find and select plays to be produced, while the education dramaturg prepares activities and materials for school groups and leads audience discussions. It is the production dramaturg—considered increasingly as a member of the artistic team that puts a show together—whose duties concern us here.

The production dramaturg is intended to be a kind of ombudsman for the play, someone with no direct stake in the production who can be an effective advocate for the script's protection during the bruising production process as well as being a devil's advocate for the director's vision, helping shape it and then helping keep it true to itself. The dramaturg is steeped in theatre history, literature, and criticism, and is there to help the director formulate an approach to the play that takes advantage of these disciplines. He or she is also there as an information resource for the other artists working on the play, and to act as a gadfly throughout the process, speaking up to the director (in private) should the production begin to lose sight of the play, or, in the case of a new play, pushing the playwright (also in private) toward script improvements.

The concerns that a dramaturg addresses have always existed, so in this sense dramaturgy is as old as theatre itself. It has always mattered that a play be as well written as possible, just as it has always mattered that it be designed and staged in a way that makes sense, and that the actors know what their characters are talking about. But the people in the theatre who have traditionally worried about these dramaturgical matters have been the playwright, the actor, the designer, and, since 1875 or so, the director.

The dramaturg as a distinct person in American theatre is a new phenomenon. It has roots in European theatre as far back as the eighteenth century, but the profession had no foothold in this country until the 1970s. Now most large theatres here, and many small and medium-sized ones, have a dramaturg. Well and good, one might say, art forms evolve as they need to evolve, and, after all, it was as recently as the nineteenth century that the director's job was brand-new.

True enough, but the director's job was created because the theatre had evolved a new task to be performed. The rise of realism required a greater attention to rehearsal and production details than the old actor-manager star system could accommodate, thus the need for an independent eye to exercise careful control over all the elements of a production was born. The Duke of Saxe-Meiningen, the first director, organized his productions around a comprehensive approach to the play. To realize this approach, he insisted on painstaking rehearsals in which he paid as much attention to crowd scenes and bit parts as to the lead roles, and carefully orchestrated the entire stage picture as it evolved moment to moment. Shakespeare and Molière, as playwrights, and Joseph Jefferson and Edwin Booth, as actors, supervised the productions in which they were involved, but Saxe-Meiningen performed a task that none of them had imagined.

Art, imitating nature as it does, abhors a vacuum. As the contemporary director has focused his or her energy on becoming an *auteur,* someone else—the dramaturg—has been brought in to do the textual work and outside research necessary to come to a profound understanding of the play.

Today's dramaturg does not perform a new task. All the fundamental issues of dramaturgy are the same today as when Aeschylus sat down to figure out which characters from the *Iliad* might make for a good play. Giving a production dramaturg something to do is a zero-sum game, and the way to play it is to take duties away from the director.*

---

*A playwright I know has asked me to point out another disadvantage to having a dramaturg around during rehearsals of a new play. This particular playwright wants to hear the widest range of feedback he can get from as many people as possible during the process, and he has found that the pool tends to dry up when there's a dramaturg. The actors and the others see the dramaturg as the official giver of feedback to the playwright (a role dramaturgs tend to promote for themselves), and feel they're expected to keep their own opinions to themselves.

This restricts the ideas available for the playwright's consideration to those of one person, and any one person's ideas are limited. (In an elegant theatre joke, Sophocles meets with his dramaturg, who says to him, "With his own mother? No one's going to buy that.") The playwright who brought this point up to me says that when he is in production on a new play, he never knows "where a good idea is going to come from—the director, actor, technical staff, ticket taker." The presence of a dramaturg inhibits this cross-fertilization and helps to distance the playwright from the production.

The Yale School of Drama seems to have been the beachhead for the profession's arrival in this country. The school describes "pre-production and rehearsal work on issues of design, direction and performance" as an important part of its degree program in dramaturgy. Would-be dramaturgs are trained to meet with the director of a play to help shape the production's approach to the play, with designers to explore visual imagery and the use of the performance space, and with actors to help them explore questions of characterization and motivation.

The Dramaturgy Pages (www.dramaturgy.net/dramaturgy), a website for working dramaturgs as well as students, spells out the job this way: "During rehearsals, a dramaturg's task is often to help the production remain in line with the vision for the production. . . . Many directors find it helpful to have a dramaturg on board who only keeps an eye on the story. . . . If a new play is still considered 'in development' during the rehearsal process . . . the dramaturg is often an intermediary between the playwright and the director," translating what each has to say into terms with which the other can work.

For any play, new or old, the Dramaturgy Pages continues, in order to "help those involved in the production better understand the piece," the dramaturg might chart out for them "the progression of the action, the activity of individual characters, the events of the play, or other elements of the action."

Arthur Ballet, one of the pioneers in the field, was dramaturg at the Guthrie Theater in the 1980s when he summed up the role of the dramaturg with what has become the profession's best-known sentence: "The dramaturg should be a resident conscience of the theatre."*

---

*The phrase *conscience of the theatre* has become enough of an embarrassment to dramaturgs over the years that nowadays it is difficult to ascertain its origin. The earliest use of it I've been able to document is Ballet's, in remarks to a 1981 conference on dramaturgy. But even by the mid-eighties, at which point it was the buzz-phrase of the profession, Ballet told an interviewer, "It's a phrase I have never used, thank God." Robert Brustein, founder of the dramaturgy program at Yale, used the phrase at around the same time as Ballet in his essay "The Future of an Un-American Activity," and to his credit has not, as far as I know, disclaimed it. Winston D. Neutel, editor of the Dramaturgy Pages web-

Where on earth is the director in all this? Why is staging a play thought to be distinct from understanding it and explaining it? How did the director come to be considered conscienceless, in need of a Jiminy Cricket to keep the production true to the play?

Oscar Gross Brockett, the great theatre historian, argues that dramaturgs are needed because directors lack the depth of training in history, literature, and criticism that dramaturgs typically have, as well as the time in a busy production schedule to discover all they need to know that might be pertinent to the play.

But it's a chicken-and-egg argument. If directors are not taking the time to research the physical, social, economic, and political worlds of the play, are not carefully defining their vision of the play so that it is rigorously true to the play's story, are not in intimate conversation with the playwright of a new play about the possibilities of the evolving text, and are not busy breaking down the play's action on paper, perhaps it's because they have been brought to believe that all of that is someone else's job. And if their undergraduate and graduate theatre programs have not given them the background to do these tasks well, perhaps the inadequacy of director training is the problem to be addressed.

Certainly even a busy director can do a complete job. Alan Schneider, in many regards my *beau ideal* of a theatre director, was famous for the meticulousness of his preparation. Best known for

---

site, wrote this response to my e-mail inquiry: "I don't know if the author would want to be identified, as every dramaturg I have heard from hates the phrase." But it pops up again in theatre essayist Martin Esslin's 1997 article "Towards an American Dramaturg": ". . . the dramaturg must be the critical and artistic conscience of the theatre; it is he/she who must apply the most rigorous yardsticks to the texts, the performance of directors, actors and designers, and to the policy of the organization in general."

Hate the phrase or not, dramaturgs tend to subscribe to the self-righteousness behind it. When asked for his job description, one leading dramaturg says simply, "I question." Another says, "My work as dramaturg (consists of) the destruction of illusionary knowledge." A third says she drops "depth charges into the psyche," while a fourth says the dramaturg "embodies the presence of consciousness . . . with which all theatremakers must come to terms." Not even Jonathan Edwards, the eighteenth-century Calvinist best remembered for his sermon "Sinners in the Hands of an Angry God," could have put it better.

his work with Samuel Beckett, he directed steadily during four decades on Broadway, off-Broadway, and at regional theatres and universities across the country. For each production he spent weeks or months—in the case of some of Beckett's plays he directed repeatedly, years—coming to a comprehensive understanding of the play and all the various worlds in which it exists. One searches his career in vain for an instance in which he appeared to be the kind of director Brockett has in mind.

Schneider was no genius and no mutant. He was a talented director who understood what his job was and worked hard at it. Any director with talent and a work ethic can do what he did.*

One argument I have heard for the presence of dramaturgs, specifically on revivals of classic plays, is that they can provide pro-

---

*Alan Schneider was known as a playwright's director, not as an actor's director. He was the favorite director of such exacting writers as Samuel Beckett and Edward Albee because of his unwavering commitment to their dramatic intentions. He was less beloved by actors, among some of whom he had an unfortunate reputation for harshness.

Albee spoke at a memorial service for Schneider, who was struck and killed by a motorcycle while crossing the street to mail a letter to Beckett, and listed what he said he had learned from the director. The list, which I have taken from Mel Gussow's *Edward Albee: A Singular Journey* (New York, 2001), illuminates the dichotomy in Schneider's professional relationships:

"Never direct a play you don't respect.

"Get to know the play you are going to direct thoroughly, long before rehearsals start.

"Hire the right actor, one capable of vanishing into a role and filling it.

"Listen to your playwright."

The points that address working with the text and the playwright speak entirely of being receptive to what they have to offer, of the collaboration as a process of discovery. This is entirely admirable. By contrast, the point about hiring the "right" actor speaks of results only: somehow the ideal person is secured and sent off to vanish into the role. Schneider undoubtedly discovered that the ideal sometimes turns out to be merely human.

Schneider's commitment to understanding and carrying out the playwright's intentions, as well as the meticulousness of his pre-rehearsal preparation, are documented in *No Author Better Served: The Correspondence of Samuel Beckett and Alan Schneider*, edited by Maurice Harmon (Cambridge, Mass., 1998). Over a thirty-year period, the two men corresponded in detail about Schneider's productions of Beckett's plays. The 450 pages of their letters provide a remarkable illustration of a healthy director-playwright relationship.

tection from directorial excess. The theory is that when a director goes overboard on a concept, the dramaturg can argue on behalf of the absent playwright and perhaps prevent the director from going too far.

This function of the dramaturg has a certain appeal, but unfortunately it is to the theatre what socialism is to economics: an interesting theory with a certain surface plausibility but no track record that suggests it actually works.

The real-life hitch is that dramaturgs work for directors. The professional dramaturg is a creature of the not-for-profit resident theatre; producers who are in business to make money have by and large not seen the wisdom of hiring someone who neither writes the play, nor directs it, nor designs it, nor acts in it, nor stage manages it, nor works as a technician on it. Dramaturgs are hired by not-for-profit theatres run by artistic directors who each want an artistic staff that will work to support, not contradict, the type of theatre the artistic director wishes to pursue.

The La Jolla Playhouse employed a dramaturg on the production of *Twelfth Night* that subordinated Shakespeare's comedy to the director's visual diatribe on the NEA's funding problems. If that dramaturg protested at all, it was to no apparent avail. The American Repertory Theatre employed a dramaturg on its production of *Endgame* that so blatantly violated the playwright's intentions that he sought an injunction against the theatre. There is no record of the dramaturg's campaign to rein in the director of that production. Nowhere in *Dramaturgy in American Theater*, a five-hundred-page anthology of mostly self-congratulatory articles, interviews, and panel-discussion transcripts by dramaturgs explaining their value to the theatre, is there a single anecdote about a dramaturg preventing a director from screwing up a play. If Trotsky had been this ineffective, Stalin would have let him live.

The argument for having a dramaturg working on the premiere of a new play doesn't even cohere in theory. Dramaturgs say their importance to a production is that they have "access to the director's ear and try to see through his or her eyes." That is to say, the dramaturg strives to achieve an intuitive sense of the director's vision of the play and to serve that vision by offering a complementary perspective on it. But dramaturgs also say they are "an advocate for the playwright," and that their job is to stand up for the integrity of the script. In a given production situation, either the director and the playwright have successfully forged a common vision of the play in production, in which case the dramaturg's perspective is merely redundant and the dramaturg's advocacy is not needed, or they haven't done so, in which case the dramaturg's twin missions are at odds with each other. How do you further the vision of a production that conflicts with the play you're supposed to protect?

In this context the dramaturg is a professional fifth wheel: not needed when the car is rolling smoothly, and not in a position to help when the alignment is out of whack.

Even the dramaturg's least controversial function, provider of research information, is a bad idea. Production research should be done by the director; handing over this task to someone else reduces its value. Ask someone to look up a word in a dictionary for you and they will bring you the definition you requested. Look it up yourself and your eye will be caught by other words and their definitions as well. You will come away having absorbed more than you went looking for. The first method is more efficient, the second is better. When a dramaturg hands a director a stack of already vetted research material, similar opportunities for random discoveries are lost. The very process of deciding which research is pertinent and which is not provides an insight into the play being researched, and the director who hands that process over to a dramaturg has diminished his or her own expertise of the play. The penalty for this will be paid in the rehearsal room when an actor's question to the director about the world of the play will have to be referred to the dramaturg for an answer.

If you aspire to do the work that the director's art requires, the presence of a production dramaturg, though intended to aid you, damages your ability to do your job well. Your natural authority in design conferences and the rehearsal room—if it is to exist at all—

derives from your mastery of the play at hand. To be sure, your technical expertise as a stager of action also plays a part, but even it will not confer authority on you unless it is clearly in the service of a broad and deep understanding of the play. This authority is inevitably weakened if someone else is seen as the master of the play.

If the involvement of another is considered necessary to keep the production true to the play, the director has become the person against whom the play must be protected.

If the director needs an intermediary to a playwright who is right there in the rehearsal room, the director is clearly not the person the playwright trusts most with the play.

Worst of all, if the cast looks elsewhere for help in understanding the text, the director has become distanced from the very task of directing.

The situation is not one of usurpation, it is one of abdication. Frequently the play should be protected from some god-awful directorial concept, and the playwright does need an intermediary, and the actors can't rely on the director to make the play clear. The dramaturg cannot be blamed for these crises, and my argument is not really an attack on dramaturgs. There are many excellent dramaturgs, just as there are many excellent designated hitters in the American League. But the designated hitter rule, because it creates an unnecessary team member, is a disservice to baseball, and the emergence of the dramaturg as a distinct position is likewise a disservice to the theatre. Independent of the performance of individual dramaturgs, it has this harmful effect: it puts distance between the director and the play.

The person to be blamed is, of course, the director. If by dramaturgy we mean a coherent approach to understanding all the various worlds of the play, certainly it is work that must be done. As the contemporary director has concentrated on the physical elements of production, concern with these elements has come closer and closer to defining for many people what directing is. But this definition ignores many necessary directorial functions. And so into the void have come talented dramaturgs to do what must be done.

This development, if unarrested, will leave the director a craftsman and not an artist. The director's job is to understand the play and to communicate it to others. If that job is handed over to another—and, bit by bit, that is exactly what is happening—the director becomes little more than Aristotle's stage machinist, responsible only for putting striking effects onstage. If you, as a director, help this development along by participating in this abdication, you will have sold your profession's birthright for a mess of pottage.

7 : Working with Playwrights

An OFT-REPEATED WITTICISM among directors is: "From now on, I'm only working with dead playwrights."

Playwrights, on the other hand, don't have a line this good about directors.

Unavoidable tensions are built into the director-playwright relationship. Imagine if a sculptor had to write out a detailed description of what the statue was supposed to look like, then entrust the actual sculpting to someone else, and you have a sense of what's at stake when one person directs a play that has been written by another.

In a healthy collaboration these tensions are productive. A director in such a collaboration approaches the play from a perspective that is sympathetic to, but distinct from, the playwright's. This perspective is frequently the first feedback the playwright receives and can be invaluable in helping to clarify a play's strengths and weaknesses. At the same time the process of being the playwright's sounding board gives a director an unparalleled insight into the life of the play.

But collaboration can easily give way to conflict, and tensions can become counterproductive if the relationship is misunderstood. The playwright who complains that his work has suffered at the hands of the director is a stock figure in the folklore of the theatre.

Even the most fabled of playwright-director relationships are not immune. "I can say only one thing," Chekhov wrote to his wife about the premiere of *The Cherry Orchard*. "Stanislavski has been the undoing of my play."

When there's trouble between a director and a playwright, it's usually not a matter of miscommunication. Even if the two of them are at each other's throat, the odds are they are communicating quite clearly. The trouble comes because they have different answers to the question, "Whose play is it?"

Here's what goes wrong. Directors have been trained to think of a production as being about the director's vision. Playwrights, on the other hand, see the production as being about the playwright's voice.

Some playwrights and directors believe that an adversarial relationship makes good art. I imagine there are some few situations where this has been true, but as a general working principle it is defective. The bedrock reason for having a director in the first place is to try to ensure that the audience's evening in the theatre will be a unity; if the director is at constant odds with the playwright, the possibility that the play and the production will be able to speak with one voice becomes unlikely.

I once heard Scott McPherson tell a group of college students about the first production of his play *Marvin's Room*. He told the story of a disagreement between him and his director, and how it was resolved.

The back wall of the set was built entirely of eight-inch-square translucent glass bricks. Through this wall the audience could see—but not clearly—the invalid Marvin in his bed. It is written into the script that at two points someone sits with Marvin and bounces light around the room with a compact mirror. This is done each time at Marvin's request; it is something he enjoys, but he doesn't have the strength to do it himself. The light is of course visible to us in the audience as it plays upon the translucent glass wall that separates us from the actors.

According to McPherson, the director wanted to change the compact mirror to a mobile of hanging crystals. Instead of shining the mirror's reflected light so that it bounced along the wall, the actor would jiggle the mobile around so that little shards of light would spray all over the wall in every direction. It would make more spectacular use of the glass wall, as the audience would see an explosion of light, not just a circle, dancing across it.

McPherson opposed the change, arguing that what appealed to Marvin was the controllable nature of one circle of reflected light. The scattering light from the jiggled mobile would necessarily be uncontrolled.

In the course of the disagreement, during which neither party gave ground, the director took the position that the final determination of stage business was his to make. This is a theory of directing that is followed more often than it is articulated, so it is worth noticing here. The argument boils down to this: the playwright's stage directions are really just suggestions. No one questions that the playwright has total control of what lines are to be spoken by the actors, but it is the director who is the final arbiter of the physicalization of the play. Whether the prop is a mirror or a mobile is less a playwriting question than a production decision, the argument goes, so it must be under the director's purview.

McPherson won the argument—or, rather, made the argument irrelevant—by inserting a line of dialogue. One character now asked another, "You know how much he likes it when you bounce the light off your compact mirror?" That settled it. Once the mirror was mentioned by one of the characters, the director had no ground to stand on.

But the director's argument is foolish on the face of it. The idea that stage directions written by the playwright are somehow severable from the rest of the play—are in fact not a true part of the play but merely some sort of discardable annotation—is absurd, but not in the funny Ionesco way. It is also condescending, in that it says the playwright can't be depended on to *see* the play clearly, only to *hear* it. For this reason it is entwined in much of the tension that can plague director-playwright relationships. Aristotle, remember, tells us that a play is an imitation of an action. It should—but doesn't—go without saying that any physical action the playwright has written to help get across the psychological action to be imitated is a part of the play. McPherson was smart enough to add a line that made the moment director-proof. *Director-proof.* The fact that such a word exists in the theatre should trouble directors more than it does.

Interpreting the play in the context of the playwright's intention does not strip the director of vision. Rather, it broadens and deepens the opportunities for that vision.

Think back to the hypothetical staging example for *Death of a Salesman*—Linda Loman bitterly discarding her wedding ring into the dirt of Willy's grave as she tells him goodbye. It is a choice that would be at odds with any conscientious understanding of the playwright's intention, but which is not explicitly ruled out by the script. Seeing it onstage would, I believe, jolt an audience. Jolting an audience is, all things being equal, not a bad thing.

Compare this to the actual staging given the same moment by Robert Falls in his production of *Salesman* at the Goodman Theatre, later presented on Broadway on the fiftieth anniversary of the play's premiere. Saying goodbye to Willy, Elizabeth Franz as Linda *lay down* in the dirt of his grave, as if to lie with him one last time. Few directors, if any, had ever staged the moment this way, yet the choice was absolutely anchored in the character as Miller wrote her. She doesn't understand everything about Willy, but her love for him passes all understanding. Her lying down in the dirt jolts the audience, but—more important—it resonates with them. A director can only make this kind of discovery about a character by living through the play with the playwright's mind. It's not that this Linda wasn't Falls's—or Franz's, for that matter—but that she remained unquestionably Miller's as well.

Whose play is it you're directing? Well, right under the title it says "by John Guare," or whomever, so I think it must be his. The director's task is to present someone else's work. The director interprets. What does that mean?

Interpretation might mean that the director says to the audience,

"Here is my best expression of what the play—this found object—means to me." Or it might mean, "Here is my best expression of what I believe the playwright intends the play—this creation of his or hers—to mean to all of us." Productions that are directed on the first basis will be successful as often as the director happens to have a personal response to the material that coincides with the point of view that the playwright has built into the play. But this approach puts the director in the position of the intuitive actor whose range is limited: if he's well cast in a role he can relate to, he'll be great; cast him outside his range and he's lost.

The second basis—"Here's what I believe the playwright intends"—is a foundation upon which more can be built. For one thing, it's a foundation that automatically includes "here's what the play means to me." No director can communicate what he or she believes the playwright intends the play to mean without the director's personal response to the play also becoming clear. But the reverse is of course not true.

If you are directing the first production of a new play, there is something more at stake than your good relations with the playwright, or even the quality of the production. The perception of the play that emerges from its first production will largely determine whether or not the play will have any future life.

When the Public Theater mounted the first New York production of Sam Shepard's *True West*, the script was dismissed by the critics as heavy-handed and obvious. It was called "exceedingly old hat" by the *New York Times*, which also condemned it for "pretentiousness" and an "inconclusive storyline." Other critics called it "two acts of tedious wrangling, recrimination, and vicious infighting" and "conceivably the least satisfactory Shepard play I have yet come across." The playwright had disavowed the production through a press statement ("I would like it to be known that the 'production' of my play *True West* at the Public Theater is in no way representative of my intentions . . ."), but it was the script that was categorized as second-rate. Nowhere in the *Times'* twelve-paragraph evisceration of the script, for instance, does it even mention the names of the director or actors. The playwright took the full hit.

It took a second major New York production of the play just twenty-one months later—an unusual event in and of itself—to salvage the script's reputation. Steppenwolf Theatre had sold out two different theatres in Chicago with its production, and so decided to roll the dice off-Broadway despite the play's earlier reception in New York. Steppenwolf's staging used exactly the same text that the Public Theater had used, but it caught the spirit of the play accurately and gave *True West* its current reputation as one of Shepard's most important plays. Even the *Times* repented: "Seeing the play in revival, one realizes that it was the production, not the play, that was originally at fault. . . . *True West*, revivified, should now take its rightful place in the company of the best of Shepard. . . ."

Inevitably the script gets blamed when a first production fails. It could hardly be otherwise. Critics and other audience members have no knowledge of the play independent of this production, so they naturally equate the two. Even when production flaws in a premiere production are pointed out, it is like naming the accessories to a crime. The playwright is held to be the main perpetrator.

This makes it especially important that the playwright's play is truly onstage for that production.

Precisely because you are not likely to catch most of the blame, you should work to ensure that the production is true to the playwright's full intentions. The most fundamental obligation you have to the playwright is this: if the play is going down in flames, make sure it's the playwright's fault. Of course, you don't want the theatrical plane to go down at all. But if it does, you want it to be because it turned out to be inherently unfit to fly, not because you crawled out and sawed off a wing. But if you take the play away from the playwright and impose your vision on it, and then it crashes and burns, no one may ever take a chance on that play again, and the playwright may never know whether it might have worked if directed properly.

This is a risk that doesn't exist when directing an established play. No matter how wretched your or my production of *The*

Oresteia or *Private Lives* or *Fences* might be, the reputations of Aeschylus and Noel Coward and August Wilson will remain secure, and those plays will continue to be produced more or less just as often as they would be if you and I had directed excellent productions of them.

For every playwright's story of a play being ruined by a director, there is a director's story of saving a script in need of help. They are the same story, told from opposite perspectives. So Chekhov thought Stanislavski had ruined *The Cherry Orchard*? Stanislavski's side of the story was that he understood the play better than Chekhov did. "This is not a comedy, nor a farce . . . ," he wrote the author, "it's a tragedy."

Bob Fosse locked Stephen Schwartz out of rehearsals and did his own rewrites on *Pippin*. The show got mixed reviews but won Fosse two Tonys and was a commercial success, which seemed (to Fosse and the show's investors) to justify his actions. George Abbott is said to have done substantial uncredited rewrites while directing Joseph Kesselring's *Arsenic and Old Lace*, which became the playwright's only hit play. Elia Kazan made Tennessee Williams rewrite the third act of *Cat on a Hot Tin Roof* to Kazan's specifications, and the play won the Pulitzer Prize.

Few anecdotes of this sort can be analyzed closely, as there is no way to know how the work would have turned out if the director had not usurped the playwright. One that can be examined in detail is the story of Kazan and Williams on *Cat*; Williams published both versions of Act Three, so side-by-side comparison is possible.

Did Kazan go too far in pressuring Williams to make changes? This is not unrelated to the question, "Which Act Three is better?" but they are nonetheless distinct questions. A close look at what happened between that director and that playwright, and at the script it shaped, goes a long way toward answering both questions.

Before Kazan agreed to direct the play, he expressed to Williams three reservations about the script, all centered in Act Three: Big Daddy was too important a character not to appear in the act;

Brick's character needed to show a dramatic progression as a result of Big Daddy's impact on him in Act Two; and Maggie the Cat needed to be made more sympathetic from an audience's point of view. Only the last of these observations struck a chord with Williams. He himself had warmed up to Maggie as he wrote her, and he wholeheartedly agreed that her charming qualities could be made more apparent.

But he did not want Big Daddy to appear in the third act, and he felt strongly that part of the point of Brick's character was his "moral paralysis," and that to have him change would be false.

"However," Williams wrote months later in a note included in the published script with both third acts, "I wanted Kazan to direct the play, and though these suggestions were not made in the form of an ultimatum, I was fearful that I would lose his interest if I didn't re-examine the script from his point of view. I did."

Williams was a soft-spoken Southern gentleman, and as such seems to have understated the extent of the conflict over the script. In his autobiography Kazan discusses what he calls "the struggle Williams and I had over the third act," and he is blunt about his "need to assert myself at all costs" and his wish to "overpower" Williams's control of the script. ("This behavior," he writes, "which would end by severing valued relationships, was unconscious.") Whether or not in the precise form of an ultimatum, Kazan communicated to Williams that his interest in directing the play was tied to Williams making it into the play Kazan was interested in directing.

Kazan was at this point the most acclaimed director on Broadway. His biggest calling cards were Williams's *Streetcar Named Desire* and Arthur Miller's *Death of a Salesman*, but he had many other hits as well, along with an Academy Award–winning film career. His name on a show was considered good for the box office. Williams, on the other hand, despite residual acclaim for *Streetcar* and *The Glass Menagerie*, was coming off three Broadway flops in a row (*Summer and Smoke*, *The Rose Tattoo*, and *Camino Real*—Kazan had directed only the last of these).

Williams wanted *Cat on a Hot Tin Roof* to be a hit, "and he wanted it passionately," in Kazan's view. Both Williams and Kazan make it clear that Williams saw Kazan's participation in the project to be vital to its success. Kazan did not hesitate to use this insecurity of Williams's to extract changes that he knew the playwright would not otherwise have considered.

Kazan's defenders in this matter say that the changes were beneficial precisely because they made the play more commercial. Broadway is a commercial venue, after all. But Kazan insists in his autobiography that the changes he wanted "had nothing to do with making the play more commercial." It was Kazan himself that was seen as the production's commercial element. The changes were the price for that element, Kazan's way of making the play his.

So Williams made the two changes in which he did not believe. Once the play was a hit, he was philosophical about the changes. "The reception of the playing-script has more than justified, in my opinion, the adjustments made to [Kazan's] influence," he wrote in the published note. But it is clear he still preferred his original Act Three. Not only did he publish it—an unusual thing to do with a preliminary draft that wasn't performed—but in the book it stands as the play's official third act; the Broadway performance version is included as a mere appendix.

Williams's position is shot through with ambiguity: I made changes I didn't like in order to keep the director happy, and I'm glad I did, but I still prefer what I wrote originally. Kazan's position on the matter—I was right, and the playwright's decision to publish both versions is an affront to me—has at least the virtue of clarity.

Williams had recognized at once that Kazan was right about Maggie needing to be made more likable, and he had no hesitation about making those changes. Kazan's insistence on the other changes, and Williams's capitulation to Kazan concerning them, guaranteed that the playwright's heart would not be in those rewrites. It guaranteed that the final version of the play as produced would be the product of an imposed vision, not an organic one.

Williams was no naif. He made the changes with his eyes open. He wanted a hit as much as Kazan did, and evidently he was persuaded that Kazan's presence on the production was more commercially viable than his own dramatic instincts.*

One of the most valuable services you can offer a playwright is to point out what you think doesn't work about the play. Everyone agrees, for instance, that the version of Maggie the Cat in the revised Act Three is better than she was in the original. But if you can't persuade the playwright by the merits of your observation, you deserve to lose the argument. To manipulate an otherwise unwilling playwright into making changes, as Kazan did, is to cross the line into abuse of power.

Any time a bad process produces a good result, it's a fluke. This was no fluke. *Cat on a Hot Tin Roof* in either version is a great play. But the changes Kazan insisted on are disimprovements. They tie the play up too neatly.

With the original Act Three in place, the play is stark: we know

---

*Would the original version of *Cat on a Hot Tin Roof* have won the Pulitzer? The question raises the most common defense of Kazan's behavior toward Williams: don't argue with success, the brief goes, the script that Kazan extracted from Williams won the biggest prize in the country. The obvious short answer to the question is, "Who knows?" But a glance at the competition that year suggests a better answer might be "Almost certainly." The only other real contender for the 1955 Pulitzer Prize in Drama, according to the prize's official history, *The Pulitzer Prizes* by John Hohenberg (New York, 1974), was *The Flowering Peach*, the last play by Clifford Odets, a playwright whose heyday on Broadway had been two decades earlier. The two-man Pulitzer drama jury had recommended the prize go to Odets but was overruled by the advisory board (an odd name for the group that actually makes the final decision). Joseph Pulitzer, Jr., new chairman of the awards carrying his family name, admired *Cat on a Hot Tin Roof* greatly and wanted the prize to go to it. He also wanted to change the prize's image as an award that went to conservative, morally uplifting plays—which is exactly what *The Flowering Peach*, a retelling of the Noah's Ark story, was—and he recognized *Cat*'s theatrical effectiveness in dealing frankly with powerful sexual themes. As *The Flowering Peach* had flopped at the box office, it was easy for the advisory board to follow its chairman, and Williams got the Pulitzer. Given an understanding of the backstage politics of the decision process, it is hard to imagine *The Flowering Peach* beating out either version of *Cat on a Hot Tin Roof*.

Big Daddy's final disposition only because we hear his offstage cry of pain and we see Big Mama rush into the room to find the morphine the doctor has left for him. Brick is as emotionally distant from Maggie as ever, so she is without the ally she needs in her battle against Gooper and Mae. This version of the play does not wrap up in a conventional manner. Loose ends—who will inherit the plantation, what will happen to Brick and to his marriage with Maggie—dangle.

The replacement Act Three alters the tone of the play considerably. Big Daddy is never hit by the pain here at all, and he enters late in the act as the others have been discussing the disposition of his estate behind his back. He makes it clear to them that he has overheard at least part of what they have said, and then affects to have nothing on his mind by telling a dirty joke. Maggie announces, falsely, that she's pregnant with Brick's child. Big Daddy believes her and exits with the announcement that he will see his lawyer the next day, presumably to leave the plantation to her and Brick. Once he's offstage, Gooper and Mae confront Maggie. They know, because they eavesdrop, that Brick refuses to sleep with Maggie and thus her claim of pregnancy cannot be true. But Brick suddenly rouses himself from his deadness and supports Maggie's claim. "This girl has life in her body," he says, meaning any number of things, perhaps not least that she has made him suddenly realize that possibility for himself as well. Maggie has spent the play asserting that she is alive, and now Brick steps forward and joins her. Gooper and Mae exit, and the play ends with Maggie and Brick in a tacit agreement to make her lie come true. Brick sits on the bed and allows Maggie to begin seducing him; she speaks of her determination—"nothing's more determined than a cat on a hot tin roof"—as the curtain falls.

The denouement in this version is neatly packaged. Big Daddy's evisceration of Brick in Act Two, plus Brick's finally admitted admiration for Maggie, has brought Brick to rejoin the living. Maggie will get pregnant. Brick and Maggie will inherit the plantation. Maggie wins.

This dramatic tidiness is at the cost of the dramatic complexity that comes with ambiguity. In the original version, nobody wins. Maggie makes her false announcement out of Big Daddy's presence, and when she is disbelieved by Gooper and Mae, Brick does not back her up. We are given no clue as to whether Big Daddy will believe her either, and he is so quickly in the alternating hands of cancer pain and morphine that it is clear he won't be seeing his lawyer the next day anyway. Most critically, there is no détente between Maggie and Brick, nor any seduction, nor her talk of determination. Instead she pleads with him that she really does love him, and the play's last line is his response: "Wouldn't it be funny if that was true?"

At the end of the original version, the future of the characters is completely murky; at the end of the revision it's crystal clear. The original has the kind of ambiguous, unsettling ending that became more fashionable during the next two decades, in the wake of Harold Pinter's and Edward Albee's work. The neatly resolved Broadway ending is more typical of successful 1950s dramas by such lesser writers as William Inge.

The Pulitzer makes it slightly awkward, perhaps, to argue that the changes done at Kazan's behest damaged the play. But the original has a richness and a riskiness that the revision lacks. Keeping Big Daddy offstage in Act Three, for instance, is strong playwriting precisely because the audience expects to see him again. His rapid deterioration is shocking to us because it defeats our expectation. As for Brick's change of heart, Williams put it best in his published note: "I don't believe that a conversation, however revelatory, ever effects so immediate a change in the heart or even conduct of a person in Brick's state of spiritual disrepair." Whatever the pluses of having Brick jump to Maggie's defense, plausibility is not among them.

What Kazan did is what any outside person almost inevitably does when trying to override a playwright's instincts about a play: pull the play toward what the outside person knows works, which is of course based on that person's sense of successful plays that already exist. Williams started out aiming at something different, but he allowed himself to be maneuvered back toward the familiar.

Throughout Kazan's account of the production process for *Cat on a Hot Tin Roof*, he stresses how he bulldozed the playwright. Williams was opposed to Kazan's choice of actor to play Maggie; Kazan "forced her on him," in his own words. Kazan says Williams also objected to the overtly presentational approach to staging that Kazan had in mind for the show; Kazan had a set designed that he knew would make any other kind of staging impossible. Williams didn't like the set, says Kazan, but had approved it early on, "when he was ready to approve of damn near anything I asked for, because I was the director he wanted." Once the set was built, "dear Tennessee was stuck with my vision, like it or not."

The implied threat of losing Kazan's services if Williams didn't acquiesce in a particular matter seems to have been a favorite tactic. The set was approved on this basis. The Act Three script changes were done because Williams came to fear that Kazan would otherwise turn the job down. Kazan actually threatened to quit during rehearsals, according to him, because Williams offered a note directly to an actor one afternoon.

Perhaps because he knew that Williams had mixed feelings about the text of the third act, Kazan prevented him from having contact with the cast. It wasn't just a question of not wanting him to give them acting notes. Williams biographer Donald Spoto quotes a *Cat* cast member as saying, "Kazan didn't want us talking about the play with the playwright."

Remarkably, the involvement of Tennessee Williams in the world premiere production of one of his plays was seen by his director as an obstacle to be gotten around.

If you and your playwright have built your relationship right, you will recognize his or her involvement in your production as an asset, not an inconvenience. A right relationship between the two of you is one in which you have striven to attain a vision of the play that is united with the playwright's. As you begin holding production conferences, auditions, and rehearsals, the playwright becomes the sounding board for you that you have been for the playwright.

In a professional situation, the playwright will almost certainly have the contractual right to approve casting. This is as it should be, but experiences like that of Williams—being pressured by a forceful director into giving approval he might have preferred to withhold—are not all that rare.

Don't cast anyone whom your playwright doesn't want in the play. There's a saying that 90 percent of both the joy and grief you encounter in life will be the result of your choice of mate. A similar statement could be made about casting a play: by far the biggest factor in the success or failure of your production will be the selection of the actors to play the roles. Once a person has been cast as a given character, most of the decisions pertinent to that character have been made. How does the character look, move, sound, and think? Until casting, the possible answers have been infinite, but suddenly the answer is that the character looks, moves, sounds, and thinks like the actor. The better the actor, the greater the range that still exists, but no actor's range is unlimited. The brute truth is that once a play is cast, most of the options for characterization have been closed off, and only a few—it is to be hoped, the right few—have been opened up.

Everyone is married to one another in this arrangement: the actor to the character; the whole cast to each other, and to the director, and to the playwright. The worst thing you can do is make it a shotgun wedding. If you are set on an actor to whom your playwright is opposed, the two of you need to sort out your differences. This is one of the values of having the playwright involved in casting. No matter how thoroughly the two of you have discussed all aspects of the play and its characters, new issues will arise and be clarified by the process of choosing the actors. Most likely the discussion will result in one of you seeing the other's point, which will allow the casting to proceed in a unified fashion. But to force an actor on a playwright is to commit a breach of faith, even if you're right about the actor.

By the same token, you should encourage the playwright to participate in production conferences. Here is where the physical realization of the play will be determined; the playwright has more at stake in what is decided at these meetings than anyone else.

Most playwrights, it's safe to say, are less familiar with the intrica-
cies of design issues than most directors (not that most directors are
experts in these areas themselves). So it would be relatively easy to
bamboozle your playwright into approving a design approach that
will take the play somewhere the playwright doesn't foresee and
wouldn't want. Kazan persuaded Williams to approve a set design
for *Cat* that consisted of a raked platform without much furniture or
set dressing on it. He knew this would force the action out toward
the audience in a nonrealistic, presentational way he says he also
knew Williams did not want.

(The irony here is that he may well have been wrong about
Williams's preference. Kazan goes on and on in his autobiography
about Williams wanting *Cat* to be "normal, realistic," and "just another day in the life of the Pollitt family." In the script itself, however, Williams describes the set he envisions in detail but adds that
it should be "far less realistic" than his description implies and ends
by comparing it to a set for a ballet—the most presentational kind of
stage performance there is—in its need to allow the actors freedom
to move and express "their restlessness, their passion for breaking
out. . . ." Had Kazan dealt with his playwright as a collaborator in
the production instead of as an opponent of sorts, he might have discovered that they agreed on more than he had imagined.)

The playwright's best protection against this sort of treatment is
to attend production conferences and be part of the discussions
about the designs, and you should encourage this.

A truism of the production process is that only the director
should speak to the actors and designers on substantive matters, and
that any comments the playwright has to offer must go through the
director. This is a well-intended rule, and in one specific application
a sensible one. But in the normal give and take of rehearsals and design conferences, it has no good place.

Certainly it is the director who bears responsibility for the production and who must be the one to articulate to the actors and designers the vision of the play shared by director and playwright.
That's the very heart of your job, after all. No playwright who is re-
spectful of your obligation to speak for the production (and you

shouldn't agree to work with the other kind) will wish to usurp you in this area, but that doesn't mean you should require the playwright to take a vow of silence.

The task of mounting the actual production is the process of giving specific articulation to the general principles upon which you and the playwright have already agreed, so the notion that the playwright has now given up aspects of the play is mistaken. In the back and forth of both design conferences and rehearsals, there may well be any number of points upon which a playwright might offer useful feedback. The acting note that Williams offered a *Cat* actor, for instance, which caused Elia Kazan to take him aside and threaten to quit if Williams ever did such a thing again, was a suggestion about the musicality in a Southern lady's vocal inflection, a matter about which Tennessee Williams could fairly be considered more of an expert than the New Yorker Kazan.

The reason for the rule against playwrights talking is to keep the lines of communication clear from the director to the actors and designers, but the frequent effect of the rule is to minimize the playwright's participation in the production. This is not a good trade-off: the actors and designers should be able to hear the playwright's comments without becoming confused about who is directing the show. A director who fears this is either unsure how to handle authority or not confident that his or her vision of the play matches the playwright's.

Let me be clear: if you and your playwright are arguing in front of the cast about large issues of the play, such as *Who's the protagonist?* and *What's the action?*, the two of you haven't done your homework together and your production is doomed. Or if your playwright keeps jumping in to contradict you publicly on minutiae, this can only hamstring your work and undermine your authority.

But there is a fertile middle ground in which playwright and director have discussed the play and reached agreement on essential matters. The director is committed to putting the playwright's play onstage, and the two of them have been articulate and specific with each other about what is intended. These two have a good working relationship already and should not fear continuing their conversation in front of others working on the show. There will likely be disagreements here and there in the course of a typical rehearsal period, as there are between, say, director and actor, but there is no reason for these disagreements to derail the show.

A sensible application of the rule about playwrights not giving notes is this: when notes are to be given following a run-through, the need for efficiency suggests that the director give the notes. No good end is served by subjecting the actors to being taken through the notes twice, with some points undoubtably being repeated and others perhaps contradicted by the two people giving them. To have the playwright disagree with you in front of the actors as you give the notes is unhelpful to all concerned. Equally so is to force the playwright to wait to discuss the notes with you until after the actors have received them and been dismissed. Before you give notes to the cast, therefore, sit down with the playwright and go through them together. Then take the playwright's notes and incorporate them into yours. This may well take some time—it may even mean you don't give notes to the actors until after the lunch break or even until the next day—but if you expect the playwright to take a back seat in the giving of notes, make sure you never surprise him or her with what the notes are going to be.

Equally important, these notes sessions with the playwright are where you will find out, every day, whether you and the playwright have differences of opinion to iron out. If so, iron them out before the notes on that topic are given to the actors.

One playwright I know met with her director regularly following rehearsals to go over notes on the day's work. She would give her notes to the director, and the director would nod and agree; but when the director passed them on to the actors the next day, they would be slightly different and no longer what the playwright had intended. Day after day the playwright made her points, and day after day the director altered them before giving them to the cast. Finally, fearful of seeing her play slip away, the playwright started giving direction straight to the actors. This was an extreme measure to take, and not recommended as it creates enormous tension for everyone, but the director left the playwright no good choice.

Don't make the same mistake. The only defense for muzzling the playwright during notes is your commitment to being a reliable spokesperson for the playwright's intentions.

The living playwright is much more useful to you than the dead one, precisely because he or she can still offer opinions. There's no need to feel threatened by this as long as the two of you continue to ground your working relationship in a common vision of the play.

8 : When Not to Direct

At any one of those all too frequent theatre conferences where theatre practitioners gather to discuss the state of the art (usual conclusion: "good") and the state of audience development (usual conclusion: "bad"), invariably a panel discusses the topic of new play development. At one of these sessions the playwright Eric Overmyer put his finger on the paternalism of the development process as it is generally practiced: "Question your assumptions. I think the main assumptions that exist in the American developmental phase of theatre are that a play needs fixing and someone besides the writer is able to do that. Question that."

The rest of the panel—dramaturgs, mostly, who make part of their living by critiquing scripts to playwrights—failed to take up Overmyer's challenge, preferring to treat him as a quaint aberration, like Elwood P. Dowd at his sister's tea party. But the director who wishes to work with new plays would do well to ask the questions that Overmyer suggested that day.

The only legitimate point of a development process is to expedite the playwright's decisions about his or her own work—not to steer the decisions, or even influence them, but to smooth the road for the playwright to make up his or her own mind. A development process succeeds if it helps a playwright diagnose the play as it exists in the present moment; too often the director allows or encourages the process to prescribe what should happen to the play in the future.

The development process has two mainstays: the reading and

the workshop. The reading, either staged or unstaged, either public or private, usually involves a time commitment of only a few hours and provides a snapshot of the play at a given moment in its journey toward completion. The workshop can last from several days to several weeks and tries to move the play along the road.

At any step of a play's development short of actual production, directing only gets in the way. You should by all means be involved in the development process, as it is an excellent way to learn about the play and because you are in a position to be valuable to the playwright. But now is not the time to interpret the play; it is the time to wed your vision of it to the playwright's. Discover the play, don't direct it yet.

A good place to start not directing is at the reading. The playwright needs to hear what the play is like, warts and all. Skillful directing tends to disguise the warts, which is why it's not wanted at this point. Hidden problems don't get fixed.

Readings are good at demonstrating one thing only: what the play sounds like. For this reason, unstaged readings are generally much more useful than the more popular staged readings. Many directors use readings to demonstrate what some hypothetical production of the play might look like, but there is usually not much developmental point to such a demonstration. Minimally rehearsed actors reading their lines cannot be expected to achieve the proper pace, characterization, or depth of meaning while they must also read their blocking notes so they can move around the stage pretending to relate to other actors who are similarly distracted. An unstaged reading, in which actors who have some familiarity with the script sit around a table with the director and playwright and simply read it out loud, eliminates these distractions. The actors are freed to concentrate on the relationships between the characters. The reading sounds better, truer to the play, which is the point.

This point is best served if the reading is not directed at all. You and the playwright should line up the best readers available for each role, and distribute scripts to the cast well in advance of the reading so that they have a chance to read the play before they arrive at the reading. There you and the playwright should answer any questions the actors may have, and then they should read the play out loud. What you want to hear is the unfiltered play, fresh from the page, and this is the way to get it.

The only good reason to do a staged reading is to give the playwright feedback from an audience. It can be difficult for an audience to follow an unfamiliar play in an unstaged reading. When all the actors are sitting together at a table, an audience member may have trouble just keeping mental track of which characters are onstage and which are offstage at any given moment.

If you direct a staged reading, direct it as little as possible. Take two minutes, tops, to sum up the play's underlying psychological action, then work through the play once to give the actors the absolute minimum blocking they'll need so that the audience can keep track visually of who is in any given scene. (One procedure that works well is to seat all the actors along the perimeter of the playing area, then bring the actors needed for each scene into center stage to stand or sit and read their scene before returning to the perimeter when their character exits the scene.) Run through everything one more time, and then be done with it.

I have seen fully staged readings that had all the detailed blocking you might expect to see in a full production, as well as lighting and sound cues, props that had to be manipulated by actors who were also carrying scripts and turning pages every minute or two, and even costume changes between scenes. This sort of reading might be appropriate when auditioning a finished play for potential producers or investors, but it has nothing to do with developing a new play. If you spend more than six hours rehearsing a developmental staged reading of a two-hour play, you're doing too much directing.

A workshop of a new play, in which the director and playwright work with a company of actors (and sometimes designers) for an extended period of time, offers a host of benefits for the play's improvement—and just as many perils. In large part, whether the play you're developing reaps the benefits or suffers the perils will depend on how you go about your job. The trick is to make sure that the playwright drives the process, and that the process does not drive the playwright.

Some years ago the *Los Angeles Times* documented the daily events of a five-week workshop of a play by an unpublished playwright with whose work I was familiar. The director of the workshop was also a playwright (in fact a Tony Award–winning playwright) who swore by the workshop process as a tool for serving the writer. But he warned the playwright on the workshop's first day, "Prepare to be violated."

Over the weeks the playwright, the director, and six actors read, staged, discussed, and did improvisations of the play. Every day the playwright brought in new pages, and twice the workshop adjourned for a week to give the playwright uninterrupted time to rewrite entire acts. The five weeks culminated in two public readings of the play, followed in one case by an audience discussion.

When its workshop life began, the play was about two men, one a restaurateur and the other a printer, both obsessed with the same woman. The playwright did not consider the play finished, but he had already spent a year writing it, had heard it in staged readings at two other theatres, and had a clear sense of what he wanted it to be.

The director's notion of attempting to serve the play by violating the writer is an apt description of his approach to the workshop. On Day One, actors who had read the play exactly once were encouraged to spout off about what changes the playwright should make; by Day Two the director had them improvising lines of their own whenever they didn't care for what was in the script. By the end of the first week, whole scenes were being improvised.

The director did a lot of directing. Working from the premise that, in his words, "the extraordinary nature of the theatre demands that plays get on their feet and get walked around and pushed around a room," he staged successive drafts of scenes as they came along, initiated improvisations intended to address the play's perceived problems, and conducted exercises in which the actors played volleyball in character. (Volleyball had nothing to do with the play—was never mentioned in the play—in any of its incarnations.) Every day the director was there, the director was busy directing.

The dominant personalities in the feedback discussions were the director and the actress playing the woman who was the object of the two men's obsessions. The actress pushed hard for changes to her character ("The scales have got to fall from your eyes," she told the playwright at one point, when he was resisting her suggestions), and by the end of the five weeks the play was about the woman finding her own way through a man's world, not about the two men who desired her.

The script started the workshop with twenty-six scenes; it finished with forty. In the workshop's last three days, the play received three different endings, none of which was favored by any of the workshop participants, including—most of all—the playwright. The director explained to friends who watched one of the endings being rehearsed: "We foisted that on him."

The outcome of this elaborate sabotage was predictable. The playwright fled the auditorium at intermission of the first public reading and didn't watch the second at all. He was embarrassed, he told the *Times* reporter, "because I knew I could write better than that." The artistic director of the theatre that produced the workshop and held an option on the script told the playwright that the play had lost the unique voice that had made it attractive in the first place. A few months later, preparing the script for a production elsewhere, the playwright threw out almost all the changes generated by the workshop and went back to the draft he had brought to it.

But the workshop was nonetheless considered a success by its other participants, one of whom said it was "thrilling to be able to duke it out with the playwright."*

---

*The *Los Angeles Times* account of the disastrous new-play workshop ran on September 7, 1986, under the headline "Theater-by-Committee: Everyone's an Author," by Barbara Isenberg. The article sparked a debate in the letters pages of the *Times* arts section that went on through October 19, as well as a

It's easy to say that playwrights should simply stand up to the kind of assault that happens so often in play workshops. True enough, and people shouldn't negotiate with terrorists either. But the director of a workshop should not be leading an assault on the play in the first place. If you do, the root problem is not that your playwright feels compelled to compromise in order to get out alive.

Just as in Greek tragedy, the great strength of a workshop carries the seeds of its own destruction. Its defining characteristic is that it rewards change. The workshop's purpose is to change the script, and a workshop tends to be judged a success or failure based on the amount of rewriting it engenders. If every day the playwright brings in new pages for the actors and director in response to the previous day's feedback, the sheer activity of all this creates the impression of productivity: when people say that a given script was torn apart and rewritten in the course of a workshop, they generally believe they are praising the workshop.

Sometimes change is good, sometimes change is bad. But in a workshop, change is always rewarded. If not much rewriting happens in the course of a workshop, the verdict is that the playwright did not take advantage of the process, though it may be that the process confirmed the playwright's preference for what was already written. In any event, workshops are not designed to reward the careful consideration that is frequently necessary to good writing of any sort; instead they reward quick turnaround. This dynamic can

---

pair of columns by the paper's theatre critic. The critic made the predictable point that both a flood of unwarranted input and no input at all are unhelpful. The letters were livelier. One called the playwright "spineless," others denounced what they called the "gang" school of playwriting. A few people affiliated with the theatre that sponsored the workshop wrote in to criticize the reporting, though none was able to specify any inaccuracies in it. The final letter printed on the subject was from the playwright, who made, in two sentences, the point I hope my chapter makes: "There is nothing inherently wrong with the process. The problem with any group creative process is in the great mix of personalities and the varying degrees of experience, talent and power each brings to the project."

make it difficult for the playwright to keep a firm hold on the play. Suddenly there are a half-dozen or more people, all of whose opinions the playwright values, speaking in various degrees of forcefulness and disagreement about how the play should go. Inevitably some workshoppers are more articulate or stronger personalities than others; their opinions will likely carry more weight and be incorporated into the script. If the play that begins the workshop is about the soccer mom, but the actor playing the team coach dominates the conversations about what to change, guess who the play might be about when the workshop ends.

A playwright can be inundated by this process if it's not managed well, and then it becomes destructive. The playwright whose workshop is described above was so frustrated by what was happening to his script that the draft he brought into rehearsal one day bore the subtitle "A Play by Eight People" rather than his own name. A workshop provides the director with an unparalleled opportunity to develop an intimate relationship with the play as a growing thing. Your approach to this opportunity will determine whether or not the workshop helps the playwright.

The director is in a better position than the playwright to control the potential excesses of the workshop process. The playwright is obliged to be receptive to whatever feedback comes down the pike. The workshop participants have been gathered on the likely presumption that the playwright is interested in anything they have to say about the play in progress, and it is impolitic at best for the playwright not to listen. If the playwright appears unwilling to consider any given piece of sincerely offered input, he or she may seem closed-minded about the play, which could in turn take the bloom off the entire enterprise. The workshop, after all, is set up for the playwright's benefit, so the playwright is expected to welcome what it offers.

Apart from political considerations, the playwright may simply have difficulty sorting through feedback instantly and objectively. Most of us have enough self-doubt that it would be easy to give in to a clearly expressed and sincerely felt critique of something about which we feel a little insecure in the first place. This is exactly why any writer needs time to reflect—but the typical workshop gives its playwright only time to rewrite.

The director should guide the feedback conversation into fruitful areas. A workshop is not a free-for-all, and letting half a dozen people bash away about how they'd write the play helps no one. This is why the tone the director sets is paramount: a director who makes it clear that the playwright is in charge of the play sets a different tone than one who declares open season.

Setting the right tone starts long before the workshop, back during your initial conversations with the playwright about the play. The rule of thumb is simple: be clear about your reactions to the play as it currently exists, but do not presume to tell the playwright how to write plays.

Limit yourself as much as possible to describing your reactions to the play: how it made you feel at various points, what it seems to be about, what you see in the characters, and so on. One excellent form of feedback is simply to summarize the play back to the playwright, so he or she can see if the plot is clear. Make observations; avoid making suggestions. An observation is an open-ended form of feedback, a suggestion is not. It's more helpful for the playwright to hear things like "I got confused in the second act because I lost track of what Tyler had done with the weapon—is that okay?" than to be told, "You should make Hazel the killer."

Observations ask for reflection. They provide a different perspective on what the playwright has written, and fresh knowledge of a different perspective encourages the playwright to look anew at the play. Suggestions ask only for acceptance. They provide no perspective at all on what has been written, other than that it has somehow been found inadequate.

These are the guidelines that should govern your conversations with the playwright about the play, and they are the guidelines you should bring into the workshop with you. "Let's not tell her how to write her play" does not sound defensive coming from the director, whereas the playwright who says, "Don't tell me how to write my play" might just as well call the rest of the workshop off. If an actor says, "I don't think my character would say (*or* do *or* wear) that," a good director should be able to steer the conversation toward the actor's understanding of the character as currently written and away from the actor's notes on what the character ought to be like. The director's job is to keep the focus on *what the play is like right now.* A good workshop is diagnostic, not prescriptive. What the play will be like in the future is the playwright's worry.

This approach to workshopping a play may result in fewer pages being rewritten in the course of the workshop, but also, I would guess, fewer rewrites being discarded in the weeks and months following the workshop. A director's responsibility to the play in development is not distinct from his or her responsibility to the finished play in rehearsal: to serve the playwright's intentions.

9 : Working Without Playwrights

WHEN YOU DIRECT A PLAY, you always collaborate with a playwright, even when there is no such person in the rehearsal hall to whom you can whisper questions. When your collaborator is, say, Lorraine Hansberry or Henrik Ibsen, your obligation to the playwright is exactly the same as when you collaborate with a playwright who is there with you: to convey the playwright's meaning. What is completely different is your means of discharging the obligation.

Without the playwright around to answer your questions, without a period of script development work to help you make discoveries, the play is essentially a fixed object, and you are on your own as you enter into it. This is the situation for most directors most of the time.

Your first step is simply to decide if you like the play well enough to want to direct it. When working directly with a playwright on a new play, you might legitimately decide to direct a show based on the unfinished play's promise, or even to direct a weak play because you believe in the playwright's potential to do better work farther down the road. But the only good reason to do a finished play in the absence of the playwright is that you think it's good, as is. Many directors will take on a bad play in the hope of making it good; it doesn't work with plays any more than with prospective spouses.

This first step sounds simplistic, I know, but it provides you with a valuable discipline. It forces you to meet the play on its terms, not on yours. If the play you're to direct is good, you must treat it as such: not as either a series of problems to be disguised or as a platform from which to launch your own agenda, but as a repository of strengths to be understood and employed.

A play creates a complete world. When push comes to shove, everything you need to make the play work is in the play. A perhaps apocryphal story about the first production of Harold Pinter's *The Birthday Party* relates that the actor playing Stanley asked Pinter what the event was in Stanley's past that brought on the events of the play. "None of your business," was Pinter's reply. Well then, the actor pressed, what happens to Stanley after he is taken away at the end of the play? "None of your business," the playwright repeated. Whether the story is true or not, its point is correct: the action *of* the play is the action *in* the play. The best preparation for directing a play—not the only preparation, mind you, but the best—is to cloister yourself off from the world and absorb and digest the play itself.*

After a period, perhaps weeks long, of reading and rereading the play and thinking about it and rereading it and thinking some more, you will almost certainly have developed a mental list of matters related to the play about which you wish you knew more. Since the playwright is not around to fill you in, now is the time to go outside the play.

Just because a play creates a complete world doesn't mean you can understand that world completely without help. Some things about the world of the play you will need to look up. What was San Francisco like in the 1930s? How exactly are all these English kings and would-be kings related? In what manner did nineteenth-century Swedes normally celebrate Midsummer's Night? Which Greek gods

---

*Some version of the Harold Pinter story is apparently true. Here is an excerpt from a newspaper profile of Alan Ayckbourn (Simon Fanshawe, "Round and Round the Houses," *The Guardian*, August 5, 2000): "In his early days as an actor, Ayckbourn was once directed by Pinter in one of Pinter's own plays. As he was feeling his way into the part, he asked the playwright, 'Where does this guy come from?' Pinter replied: 'Mind your own fucking business.'"

are the Dioscuri, and why should they care about Orestes? These are all practical questions, and if you are directing the plays to which they relate, you will need to make the answers clear onstage.

This level of research is the most valuable you can do, precisely because it is rooted in making the action of the play—not the theme of the play, or the production history of the play, or the background of the playwright, but the action of the play—clearer to you. It doesn't tell you what you should think, it provides the information you need in order to make up your own mind.

Another worthwhile use of your time is to read other plays, and other writings in general, by your playwright. This is a good idea even if you are working directly with the playwright, but if you are not, it is your only means of direct contact with his or her mind. *My Children! My Africa!* sheds light on *The Blood Knot*, as *Exit the King* does on *The Chairs*, as *Top Girls* does on *Cloud Nine*. A good playwright has a consistent voice, and insight into any one of his or her plays can be strengthened by familiarity with the others. *Our Town, The Skin of Our Teeth,* and *The Matchmaker* share little by way of style or structure. But each could only have been written by Thornton Wilder, and the director of any of them would do well to know the others.

So far this research is primary: direct research into the actual text itself, and direct exploration of the playwright's writing. Of more dubious value is secondary research into other people's opinions of the playwright and the play.

Researching the playwright's personal background might, to a limited degree, help you understand the play's action and characters, but bear in mind that understanding the playwright is not the goal. Your job is to put Edmund Tyrone onstage, not Eugene O'Neill. And in any event, a given play probably sheds more light on the playwright than the biography sheds on the play. You could gain a decent impression of the concerns of, say, Tom Stoppard by reading his plays, but even a close study of his youth and education and marriage (if in fact he has had one, or several) would not help you stage *Travesties* or *Arcadia*.

This is equally true for plays that seem clearly autobiographical.

If you were to read an account of Tennessee Williams's early life, for instance, you would undoubtedly encounter passages that bring *The Glass Menagerie* to mind. But any points in that account that seem to you to strike home will do so because they are already in *Menagerie*. Whenever the biographer's interpretation of events or personalities diverges from the events and portrayals in the play, they are beside the point; whenever they agree with the play, they are redundant to an understanding of the play itself. Neither *oh, this really happened this way* nor *gee, the play isn't true to life at all* is pertinent to the play as a work of art, any more than it matters whether the model for Michelangelo's *David* was really that good-looking.

Any good play stands free of its playwright's biography: Shakespeare's plays stand in the absence of much reliable information about his life at all. So go ahead and read the biographies of your playwright if you wish, but remember this: if the playwright were here and working with you on your production, the two of you would talk about the play, not about his or her childhood.

The production history of your play, or of plays like it, is of limited value to you as you plan your own production, and may inhibit your ability to achieve an original perspective. I do not wish to be misunderstood on this point: a good working knowledge of theatre history is essential to good directing. You need to know, for one example, that Shakespeare wrote his plays for theatres in which there was little scenery and structured his action to flow continuously on and off an open stage. If you know this you won't kill the rhythm of your Shakespeare production by stopping the play intermittently for lengthy scene changes. It is worth knowing, for another example, about the argument between Chekhov and Stanislavski as to whether Chekhov's plays are comedies or tragedies as you form your opinion of, say, *The Sea Gull*. But sometimes the received wisdom of others prevents a director from seeing the play independently.

Greek tragedies are frequently—perhaps even typically—produced with at least some of the actors wearing masks. There is no good reason for this. No character and no member of any chorus in any Greek tragedy wears a mask. But the actors playing them frequently do so because the Athenian actors who originally performed these plays wore character masks. The thinking, I assume, is that masks therefore make the play more authentic and are truer to its spirit. But the ancient Greeks used masks for purely practical reasons that don't pertain to the modern theatre. Only two or three actors played all the nonchorus roles in each play, so masks helped the audience keep track of who was who at any given moment. Also, their masks had exaggerated features and built-in megaphones to ensure that they could be clearly seen and heard in the fifteen-thousand-seat amphitheatre in which they performed. The masks helped the Greeks make the plays immediate and accessible; twenty-five centuries later, when a full-sized cast performs in intimate relation to an audience of a few hundred, masks have the opposite effect.

But many modern directors of these plays are misled into putting their actors into masks, for reasons that have to do with adhering to or commenting on outside research, and not with the action of the play at hand.

There are plenty of similar cases. In a tradition attached to *She Stoops to Conquer*, the character Tony Lumpkin plays with various toys during scenes, though no such business is suggested in Oliver Goldsmith's script. It was fastened onto the character early on as a way to demonstrate his immaturity, and is sometimes still included in modern productions of the play, short-circuiting the need to explore the character afresh. Likewise *Peter Pan's* title role has been played onstage almost exclusively by women, in J. M. Barrie's play and various adaptations, ever since Nina Boucicault originated the role in 1904. I know of one modern adaptation, produced by a theatre in an academic setting, that cast a male student as Peter, but all the play's widely known commercial presentations over the decades have chosen to have him played by adult women. This is despite the fact that the character is clearly male and that the play explores his relationships as a boy with three females: a substitute mother (Wendy), a tomboy (Tinker Bell), and a *femme fatale* (Tiger Lily). Casting a young-looking male gives the play a truer dynamic, but the tyranny of the play's production history will probably always work against that happening.* And innumerable productions of *Death of a Salesman* have more or less copied Jo Mielziner's groundbreaking set design from the first production and saved themselves the trouble of an original approach.

In each of these cases, and so many others, a sense of production history has replaced a sense of the play. The individual choices may be good or bad, but the point is that inheritance is not as interesting as discovery. The great achievement of Peter Brook's historic production of *A Midsummer Night's Dream*, with its trapezes and abstract white setting, was to shake off the cobwebs of romanticism that had clung to the play since the nineteenth century and allow audiences to see the play in a fresh light. The accumulations of the play's production history had obscured the play itself, and Brook swept it clean.

The production based on standard interpretations risks triteness. Its director may feel that the production has been given a kinship to important previous productions of the play, but in fact it has been made akin to the high school production of *The King and I* that puts its male lead in a bald skullcap so that the kid will look like Yul Brynner.

Least valuable is research into whatever critical theories may have attached themselves to your play. These may be interesting reading for their own sake, but avoid them whenever you are directing a play they discuss. The opinions of Jan Kott or Ruby Cohn or Eric Bentley may be sensible or foolish as they pertain to the play you are to direct, but you are in no position to judge until you have come to your own point of view about the play. Primary research enables you to find your own way into the play; secondary research into the opinions of others detours you from your path and brings you into the play via someone else's route. Lazy directors use this as a shortcut; they direct from a point of view they have adopted rather than developed.

---

*A detailed look at the gender issues of *Peter Pan*, both in the script and in the play's casting history, is contained in Linda Jenkins and India Cooper's article "Peter Pan: The Women in His Life" (unpublished).

C. S. Lewis argued that literary criticism in general is never terribly useful as a means of better understanding a given work, because it is our sense of the work that illuminates the criticism, not vice versa. The work can be appreciated on its own, without the critic's opinion; the critic's opinion can only be given proper weight by those who know the work. "If we have to choose," Lewis wrote, "it is always better to read Chaucer again than to read a new criticism of him." Insert the name of your playwright into that piece of advice, let the books of criticism gather dust, and read the play again.

10 : The Windowpane

Throughout these pages I have rejected the position that theatre can be primarily the director's art as distinct from the actor's. Nor do I believe that the text of the play is raw material for the director's self-expression. The director's proper role is that of the interpretive artist who communicates, precisely and vividly, the vision of the theatre's only creative artist—the playwright—to the group of interpreters—the actors—who bear ultimate responsibility for communicating that vision to the audience.

Is my position essentially conservative? Certain things ought to be conserved, and in this regard good art is no different than clean water or political liberty. Changes that are likely to result in bad art, or undrinkable water, or political oppression, ought to be opposed. New is not automatically the same as improved.

Conservative is sometimes considered the opposite of *daring, fresh,* and *innovative,* but this is surely a mistake. The opposites to those words are *cowardly, stale,* and *hackneyed,* and we all agree that these are qualities good theatre must avoid. The opposite of *conservative* (setting aside its purely political sense) is *wasteful.*

What is wasted when the director's job is distorted? As I have tried to show, sometimes the play itself is allowed to slip away, and sometimes the work of the actor—which ought to be the center of the theatre—is obscured or stifled. Always wasted to one degree or another is the opportunity for the director to bring to life a theatre that is larger than what the director brought to it, that transcends what anyone can control, that lives and grows onstage every night.

What George Orwell wrote about good prose could be said of good directing for the stage: it is like a windowpane, effective only when it invisibly enables us to see something else clearly. "One can write nothing readable," according to Orwell, "unless one struggles constantly to efface one's own personality."

The same challenge faces the director of a play. If the audience notices—stops to think about—the directing, the directing is wrong.

This is not an argument against style. It would not be possible for a talented director's production to show the play clearly without revealing something of his or her own character, any more than an essay by Orwell is likely to be mistaken for one by James Thurber. It is an argument against putting one's self in the forefront. The goal of the director's art is not self-expression but self-effacement.

That is to say, the correct approach to the director's job goes against the grain of most people who are temperamentally inclined to work in the theatre. This is why, at bottom, there is so much bad directing.

I wish to be clear about the word *bad.* Incompetent directing—bad in the sense of lacking craft—is not as rare as it should be, but over time most directors who fail to grasp even the basics are weeded out of the profession by their own repeated failures, and they need not concern us here. It is arrogant directing—bad in the much more profound sense that it damages plays and oppresses actors—that is the subject of this book.

Directors want their work to get them noticed. This is how careers happen, after all. And it is easier to get noticed by exploding a play than by interpreting it.

So why bother with what this book has to say?

The only reason is that directing is supposed to be an art form.

Directing a play is a curious art form, to be sure. It consists merely of enabling a group of other artists to express the focused intentions of yet another artist, who is probably not even present. But it is an art form nonetheless, and if you take it up, you have an obligation to be true to it.

All theatre vanishes the second it's over. But a production has a better chance of continuing to resonate with some portion of its audience, even years later, if its director has gotten inside the play and made its heart and soul clear, than if its director has stayed outside the play and used it for his or her own purposes. A classical production, for instance, that is about the director's attitude toward a current political issue will seem dated as soon as the issue fades. But one that is about the living play itself, and is successful in plumbing the depths of what that means, has the potential to be a permanent touchstone for a member of the audience.

A career in the theatre consists of the struggle to make something that is evanescent resonate. Your task in this noble pursuit is that of the lover in love, or of the faithful in worship: to lose yourself in the pursuit of the object, and thereby to be—liberatingly—true to yourself.

Appendix:
Analyzing a Play,
Demonstrated

A POINT Sherlock Holmes never tired of impressing upon Dr. Watson was that only the facts will lead you to the truth. "It is a capital mistake to theorize before you have all the evidence," he would say. "It biases the judgment. You find yourself insensibly twisting facts 'round to fit your theories."

The task of analyzing a play's action is difficult in and of itself, but it's made more so by the distractions of theme and character. Deciding too soon what a play *is about*—the theme of the play—can bias your decisions about what *happens in* the play—its action. By the same token, making decisions too early about who the characters are—how they feel about things and what they are capable of—can color your perception of what they actually do.

There will be plenty of time for these other essentials. They proceed *from* the action, and it is a capital mistake to theorize about them before you have examined the evidence properly. But an understanding of the action—to the exclusion of every other facet of the play—is the rock upon which your production must stand.

A detailed example may be clarifying. The amount of detail to be examined is part of the point to be made, but as a painstaking analysis of a single play would likely break the flow of the book proper, I offer it here as an appendix.

Edward Albee's play *Who's Afraid of Virginia Woolf?* is a widely misunderstood play in some ways; these misunderstandings can be cleared up by a careful analysis of the play. At first glance it is easy to see the play as merely an increasingly vicious battle between George and Martha, a game in which the stakes are raised and the tactics grow uglier, until George comes up with the knockout punch. This theory of the play is facile, inadequate to the breadth of the play's concerns because it is not based on a careful examination of what actually happens in it.

Nonetheless a quick search on the Internet will display an assortment of critical commentary on the play that confirms this view of the play. Myron Matlaw, author of *Modern World Drama: An Encyclopedia*, writes that the play centers on "a marriage marked by mutual hatred" and discusses "their increasingly sadistic arguments and behavior" played out in front of Nick "and his barren wife" Honey. A synopsis of the play provided by a European university for students studying American literature explains that George and Martha "engage in a harrowing battle to destroy each other . . ." and that the games they play are "seriously playful imitations of the social games we play in our everyday life." A review of the film version by Damian Cannon, proprietor of the well-regarded website "Movie Reviews UK," describes the ending this way: "In the final act George wants everyone to play a final game . . . where he can drop the final bombshell. The emotional fallout from this is intense and *somehow* [emphasis added: the use of the word betrays the fact that the reviewer doesn't follow the connection between cause and effect at this point in the action] gives rise to an exhausted calm. . . ."

These quotations, selected as typical, sum up how the play is often seen, which is also to say how it is often directed and acted. They reflect a view of the play that is shallow in its overview and downright mistaken in many of its specifics. Far from being barren, for one example, Honey is in fact pregnant, as we shall see. And I hope I am never the dinner guest of anyone who considers George and Martha's behavior to imitate everyday social interactions.

If the play is nothing more than a three-act fight between a domineering wife and an emasculated husband who finally figures out how to fix her once and for all, it is a psychological slugfest with no real meaning.

Analyzing a play's title is not usually the place to start, but Albee has given us four titles to examine, and doing so reveals something worth noticing about the play's structure. Besides titling the play, Albee has titled each of the three acts. The play title, of course, is taken from the song George and Martha heard at the party and sing to each other throughout the play:

> Who's afraid of Virginia Woolf,
> Virginia Woolf, Virginia Woolf?
> Who's afraid of Virginia Woolf,
> Early in the morning?

Virginia Woolf was a British novelist and literary critic during the first half of the twentieth century. Her name works as the sort of jokey reference that academic types would use to parody "Who's Afraid of the Big, Bad Wolf?" George and Martha sing this song, at first mockingly and, finally, tenderly. By the end of the play—which is indeed early in the morning—the question in it has taken on a highly specific meaning for them. The last line of the play is Martha's answer: "I am, George. I am."

We will have to come back to the question of what this meaning might be. We don't have enough information yet. But the act titles are more immediately helpful. Act One: "Fun and Games." Act Two: "Walpurgisnacht." Act Three: "The Exorcism."

"Fun and Games" is pretty clear. We all know what both those things are.

The word "Walpurgisnacht" is less clear. So we look it up. The encyclopedia tells us that the word derives from Saint Walpurgis, a ninth-century English nun who was a missionary to Germany. She is the patroness of protection against witchcraft, and one of her feast days is May 1. According to German tradition, the night before

May 1 is Walpurgisnacht, when all the witches commune with the devil. They conduct a satanic Mass which culminates in the ritual sacrifice of a human baby.

"The Exorcism" was originally to be the title of the entire play until Albee saw the question "Who's afraid of Virginia Woolf?" written on a wall somewhere. (And people say graffiti isn't art.) An exorcism, of course, is the procedure by which a person's body is cleansed of the presence of evil spirits.

Thanks to these subtitles, we have — before we read a word of the actual play — a general sense of how the playwright has structured the action. Fun and Games, Walpurgisnacht, The Exorcism: uninhibited exuberance turning into something ugly and debased, then leading to a final cleansing. Already we're at odds with the idea of the play as a perverse version of *Rocky* featuring Martha as Apollo Creed.

Plot

George and Martha are by themselves at the top of the play, so we see that the combative nature of their relationship is constant, not something they will put on when Nick and Honey arrive. We learn in this part of the play that George and Martha have been at a party at Martha's father's, and that Martha has invited Nick and Honey, whom she met there, over for late-night drinks. Two details that will be important later emerge in this early scene. The first is that George knows Martha's description of Nick before she finishes it: ". . . and good looking. . . ." The other is that George warns Martha, "Don't start in on the bit about the kid."

Now is a good time, just before Nick and Honey arrive, to ask ourselves the Passover Question. *Why is this night different from every other night?* In this play, as in every play that works, there is a reason why the events of the play happen. Some event, or confluence of events, has occurred that now makes the events of the play inevitable. The plague has descended upon Thebes. The auction of the cherry orchard has been scheduled. Lear has decided to retire.

Felix Unger's wife has finally thrown him out. The events of any good play are a moment of profound crisis or it would not be an interesting play to watch. It's too early in our reading of this play to say what has brought this on for George and Martha, but it's the right time to start asking the question.

Once Nick and Honey are in the door and all four are making chitchat, George has trouble finding feet for his animosity. First he attacks Nick, trying to lead him into saying something pretentious about the abstract painting on the wall so he can mock him for it; but he is obliged to apologize. He turns to attacking Martha, about her taste in liquor and the way she laughs, and is allowed to do so. Then he attacks Martha's father and is corrected by the others, all three of whom find Martha's father to be a wonderful man. Notice that when Honey asks Martha to show her where the bathroom is, Nick asks Honey, "Are you all right?"

Alone with Nick, George launches a sustained attack. We find that Nick is in the biology department while George is in the history department. George accuses Nick of being behind a plot to control the future through biological tampering with chromosomes. And George assures Nick that his and Martha's attacks on each other are just Fun and Games: ". . . we're merely walking what's left of our wits."

Other key details in this scene: George asks Nick his age and is told "twenty-eight." A few minutes later George disparages Nick's youth by saying, "You're twenty-one!" and Nick corrects him: "Twenty-eight." Also, George never addresses Nick by name in this scene but twice calls him "my boy."

Honey reenters and announces that Martha will be down as soon as she finishes changing. She also says that Martha has told her that George and Martha have a son and that he turns twenty-one tomorrow. The stage directions say that George is "incredulous" that Martha is changing, and that he wheels "as if struck from behind" when he hears that Martha has told Honey about The Son. He then tells Nick that Martha is changing for him ("Martha hasn't changed for *me* in years") and that they mustn't leave.

Martha enters, dressed extremely voluptuously. She proceeds to hit on Nick and to disparage George's manliness. George leaves the room briefly and returns with a shotgun that he fires at the back of Martha's head. It's not real: a Japanese paper parasol sprouts from the barrel when he fires it. Martha laughs it off and returns to hitting on Nick: "No fake Jap guns for you, eh?"

Nick leaves briefly, and it is worth noting here the dog that doesn't bark. When George and Martha are left alone together with Honey, neither of them attacks her in any way. They make what is, for them, polite chitchat. This suggests what will become obvious later, that there is something recognizably pathetic about Honey, something that makes her seem not worth the trouble of hurting. If George and Martha were the sadists they are accused of being, they would pounce on the opportunity to destroy a weakling.

When Nick returns, Martha hits on him again, and George calls Nick a threat because he represents the future. Martha raises the question as to whether The Son is really George's because The Son's eyes are green like hers and her father's. George says he's sure the boy is his. Martha says—and George seems to agree—that George hates Martha's father because of George's own shortcomings. George leaves to get more liquor.

In his absence, Martha tells Nick and Honey about her annulled marriage to the lawn boy at her finishing school. She is telling about marrying George as he returns: how it was assumed he would rise in the department and therefore be a good catch. George tries to prevent her from going on about his failure to rise. She taunts him and shouts the word "flop" at him. He breaks a bottle. Honey runs out to vomit, Nick follows her, and Martha follows them. George is alone onstage as the act ends. Fun and games are over.

Walpurgisnacht begins with the women offstage, and George and Nick calling a truce. Nick tells George the story of his marriage to Honey. They thought she was pregnant. By the time they realized she wasn't, they were married. George tells a story about a boy he knew who accidentally killed his parents, was put into an asylum, and hasn't uttered a sound for the thirty years since. George eggs Nick to discuss the fact he's revealed, that Honey's family has money, which Nick has halfway acknowledged to have been a partial reason he married her. George tells Nick that he has drawn Nick out on these matters in order to gather ammunition. And the truce is called off.

Martha brings Honey back from vomiting. Honey explains that she vomits easily for no reason, and that, for instance, she had a bout of it just before they were married. Martha and Nick dance suggestively while George and Honey sit. Martha tells Nick the story of George's novel, apparently the story of the boy who killed his parents that George had told Nick earlier. When she tells how her father threatened to fire George if he published the book, George rips the record from the record player and yells, "I will not be made mock of!" The others all laugh at him. Martha tells of George pleading with her father that it's not really a novel, that he himself is the boy who killed his parents. George grabs Martha by the throat and tries to strangle her. Nick pulls him off and throws him on the floor.

George, deeply humiliated, announces that it's time to play Get the Guests. He relates what he says is the plot of his second novel — actually the story Nick told him earlier, about Honey's father being a crooked preacher and about Honey's false pregnancy. Honey realizes that Nick has betrayed her privacy, and she runs out to vomit again. Nick follows Honey out, vowing revenge on George: "I'll be what you say I am." George replies, "You are already . . . you just don't know it."

Left together again, George and Martha declare total war. George says that Martha has lost touch with reality completely. He tells her — the stage direction says *"with some awe"* — "You're a monster . . . you *are*." Martha keeps saying "SNAP! It went snap," meaning that she's reached the point where she doesn't care anymore, about George or anything. Once they agree that this means "total war," the stage direction says they seem *"relieved and elated."*

Nick enters with the news that Honey is lying on the bathroom floor, and he asks for ice to give her. George goes to get some. Martha starts to seduce Nick. George comes back and they stop; George reports that Honey is asleep in the bathroom, so they use the ice to make drinks. George announces that he is going to sit and read a book, affecting not to care what the two of them might do.

This affectation enrages Martha, and she repeatedly threatens to take Nick off and have sex with him. George continues calmly with his book. Martha and Nick leave.

Now George is alone onstage, and because there is no one to be deceived, we can be sure he is not lying. At first George tries to hold on to his pretense of indifference, reading aloud a passage from his book. Then he stops and hurls the book across the room with, the stage direction says, *"all the fury he has been containing within himself."* The book crashes into the doorchimes.

(Here's a digression. The quote George reads aloud, unidentified in the text, is from *The Decline of the West* by Oswald Spengler. The book was written in 1918 and published in the United States in 1926, but an abridged edition received new attention in 1962, the same year this play was written. So it would likely be this new edition that George is reading. The book's thesis is that every culture passes through a life cycle similar to that of human life, with an adolescence, a middle age, and so on. Spengler draws parallels between modern America and ancient Carthage, positing the United States as a sort of new Carthage: George and Martha's town is named New Carthage.

Better yet, Spengler says the two principal axes for behavior in these two societies are power and money. Power, of course, is what Martha's father holds over George, and is a major reason why George married Martha; money, on the other hand, is what Honey's father holds over Nick, and is a major reason why Nick married Honey.

Best of all, Spengler describes George and Martha perfectly when he says that both Carthage and America have been led by this combination of money and power to a brutalism and a sterile intellectualism in which "children do not happen . . . because intelligence at the peak of intensity can no longer find any reason for their existence.")

Honey has been awakened by the book hitting the doorchimes, and she enters, still under the spell of a dream about giving birth. She cries as she yells at the imaginary people attending her imagi-

nary birthing, or maybe at the babies trying to be born: "GO 'WAY . . .
I DON'T WANT . . . ANY . . . CHILDREN. . . ."

George realizes that she must be pregnant, and that's why she is
throwing up all the time. He also realizes that her premarriage "hys-
terical" pregnancy was real, and that she must have aborted the fetus
somehow. Remember this is 1962 and there is no legal abortion in
the United States. "How do you make your secret little murders
stud-boy doesn't know about, hunh?"

George starts to rant at Honey, whom he knows can't really follow what he's saying, about what Martha and Nick are up to. But
Honey insists she only wants to know who it was that came to the
door and rang the bell. This gives George the idea he's been looking
for, and in a burst of inspiration he tells Honey it was a telegram
being delivered with the news that The Son is dead. Honey is horri-
fied. As Walpurgisnacht ends, George rehearses telling Martha the
news. The stage direction says *He begins to laugh, very softly. It is
mixed with crying.*

Martha is alone at the top of the third act (The Exorcism), and
so again we know the truth is being spoken. She speaks of her
sadness over what's happened to her and George ("We both cry
all the time . . ."). Nick enters. It is revealed that they didn't have
sex after all, because he was too drunk to sustain an erection.
Martha holds him in contempt for this. She says George is the only
man who's ever made her happy. She eulogizes George in the
most beautiful language in the whole play. Nick says he doesn't
believe her, and she mocks his disbelief. The doorbell rings, and
she humiliates Nick into answering it: "Can't you get the latch up,
either?"

It is George at the door, with snapdragons he has picked in the
yard as a bouquet: "Flores para los muertos," he chants. He pretends
to mistake Nick for The Son come home for his birthday. He announces that there will be one more game: Bringing Up Baby. He
makes Nick go get Honey to play this game with them.

Martha pleads with George that they not play this last game. He
not only insists they do so, he pulls her head back by the hair and

slaps her five times to make her mad. It works; as Honey and Nick reenter, the stage direction says that Martha paces and actually looks a bit like a fighter.

George launches into the tale of The Son by way of attacking Martha. She takes the bait and takes over the story, telling an idyllic version of The Son's childhood: what a healthy infant he was, how much he loved to play in the sun, and so on. George interjects Latin prayers for the dead throughout her tale. They trade opposing versions of which parent it was that The Son really loved, and their argument crescendos.

George announces to the group that a telegram has come saying that The Son has been killed in a car crash. Martha is devastated and screams that George cannot decide such a thing alone. They argue about whether George has broken the rules of the game, but he is immovable and she realizes she is powerless. Nick realizes that The Son is the ultimate game they play, and that there is no such person in reality. George tells him and Honey to leave, and they do so quickly.

The stage direction says the playwright wants this last scene played softly and slowly. George asks Martha if she wants anything and if she's tired. She makes barely any response, and then, after a long silence, she asks him brokenly if he had to do what he did. He says yes, it was time. They agree that they don't really know how things will be now. Martha starts to raise the possibility that they could—what?—have another pretend child?—but George cuts her off before she can finish the thought, and she drops it. He touches her and sings, "Who's afraid of Virginia Woolf, Virginia Woolf, Virginia Woolf . . . ?" She says, "I am, George. I am." He nods, and the play is over.

Character

The easiest trap to fall into when approaching this play is to see George and Martha as protagonist and antagonist. The play is more complex than that. George's action toward Martha is ultimately redemptive. He does what he does to save her, and to save himself. He is battling something other than her. That's not always clear even to them, but it's still true. If the marriage is really built on mutual hate, George cares only about winning the game and destroying Martha, and he can't possibly do what he does at the very end of the play. By the same token, if Martha hated George she would not accept him at the end of the play; with The Son dead, she would have no reason to do so.

They love each other. It is themselves they hate. This is what Martha means in Act Three when she says that George "has made the hideous, the hurting, the insulting mistake of loving me and must be punished for it." Neither can give openly to the other because neither feels worthy of the other.

It seems to me that each has taken on the individual blame for their shared failure to have children. Each feels like the one who has failed the other. They've replaced sex with the elaborate confrontational games they play with each other. These games even have a sexual rhythm: mounting fury building to a crescendo, followed by tenderness.

George is trying to destroy not Martha but The Son. The Son is what propels the play. The play happens because George and Martha choose to believe in The Son, just as surely as it reaches its crisis and climax because George decides to destroy that belief.

Here is the answer to the Passover Question. This night is different from every other night because it is the night before The Son's twenty-first birthday. That makes this night crucial for George and Martha. They have set rules that require them to treat their imaginary child exactly as if he really existed. It has now been twenty-one years since they made him up. He is reaching his majority, and they are losing their little boy. Although they will still be able to pretend he exists, they will have to begin inventing adult concerns for him: a home somewhere else, a career, a spouse, a whole life that is not built around them. It is impossible to believe that they, especially Martha, would want this. If they are to be true to the game, they will no longer be able to play it. No matter how they spend this night, the game will be effectively over when they wake up in the morning. To put off tomorrow, Martha has decided to make tonight last as long as she can. So she has invited Nick and Honey over for drinks.

Nick, of course, has been selected to be The Son for the evening. He doesn't know this, but George and Martha do. This is why Martha desires him and George resents him. George, remember, anticipates Nick's description when Martha first mentions him; after Nick arrives, George repeatedly calls him "my boy" and thinks he's twenty-one. Both George and Martha look at Nick and see in him the energy, ability, and strength of will to collect on the promises of life that abandoned George decades earlier. George doesn't want to see his son surpass him professionally, personally, or sexually, and Nick is poised to do all three. For most of the play, George considers Nick the real enemy. He attacks Nick because he doesn't want to see his son grow up. Finally he realizes that he has confused the symptom with the disease, and he goes after the "real" Son.

The basic story in this play is the same as in Mary Shelley's novel *Frankenstein*. Like Frankenstein's monster, George and Martha's imaginary son was created to gratify the egotistical need of his creators, but now he controls the lives of those he was intended to serve. Like Victor Frankenstein, George must kill his unnatural offspring in order to save himself.

Martha is luckier than Elizabeth, Victor's bride, who was destroyed by the monster before her husband could save her. George kills The Son not out of revenge or to score points against Martha but to force her to confront the truth. Only if they give up The Son do they have a chance of escaping the sick need for a life of illusion they have built for themselves. George attempts the gradual disintegration of illusion in their life together; he begins by shattering the one that is central. It is a step toward health and wholeness. It is not sadistic or spiteful or any of the other things it is generally considered to be. It is an act of love.

Thought

The theme? Remember, good plays don't make statements, they ask questions. This question is in the title. By the end of the play, when Martha finally answers the question, it means this: who's afraid of living life without illusion? In A *Room of One's Own*, the real Virginia Woolf wrote, "Why, if it was an illusion, not praise the catastrophe, whatever it was, that destroyed illusion and put truth in its place?" Is such a life without illusion the Big Bad Wolf that we all fear? Could any of us bear to see ourselves and our lives with the dreams rubbed off? Who knows? That's why it's a good question for a play to ask.

But this play also makes a statement, and by doing so it demonstrates why plays aren't very useful vehicles for statements.

Albee is aiming at a political statement, as the references to *The Decline of the West* make clear. If all countries pass through an arc similar to that of a human lifetime, then Albee is saying that America is mired in the same need for self-deception that George and Martha are. That's why they have the same first names as the Washingtons, to make them the ultimate emblematic Americans.

Albee once told Studs Terkel on the radio that the choice of his lead couple's names was intended as a hint to audiences to pay attention to the play's political content: "If anyone wanted to see them as representing the principles of the American Revolution with the illusory offspring of it, that was just dandy with me. Not too many people did bother to find that."

But the customer is always right, and Albee's complaint about his audience misses the point. Interpreting elements of this particular play metaphorically is a game that goes in as many different directions as there are players, and no given direction seems to lead us home.

For example, Nick has the same name as the man who was Soviet premier when the play was written. If George and Martha are the U.S.A. and their imaginary child is America's self-deceptive legacy, are Nick and Honey the USSR? And if so, what is represented by their string of aborted fetuses: failed Five-Year Plans? Or are Nick and Honey supposed to represent the younger generation of Americans to whom the torch is being passed (remember the era in which the play was written), and the message is that they will simply turn into George and Martha? Both of these theories about Nick and Honey are frequently tossed around, sometimes simultaneously by people who don't seem to realize they can't both be true (if either of them is). In fact, various points from the play (which I will not bother to list) do seem to support one or the other.

Does it even matter? How would either answer change the way the actors playing Nick and Honey play their scenes, or affect the way the audience reacts to them as characters?

The point Albee misses is that this kind of thematic puzzling over metaphoric statements is interesting and fun, but of limited value. It's useful only if it is absolutely grounded in a moment-by-moment understanding of the play's action and leads to a new and valid way of looking at the play in production.

What holds an audience is the sight of a human being making a difficult choice at a time of great crisis. No one ever leaves a theatre humming the metaphors.

Perhaps one day some brilliant director will find a way to give Albee his wish (if indeed it is his wish—the productions of his play that he himself has directed have not been apparently political) and stage this play in a way that illuminates its action from the standpoint of geopolitical critique. That could be fascinating, but it is not necessary. The play's symbolic statement is not what has made the play last; its question about human behavior has done that.

Index

Fictional and dramatic characters are included in this index only when they are discussed or mentioned independently of the work in which they appear. Characters mentioned in the context of discussing an indexed work are not included.

A NOTE ON THE AUTHOR

Terry McCabe has directed plays professionally in Chicago since 1981 and since 1988 has been a member of the theatre faculty at Columbia College in Chicago. He can be reached by e-mail at TPFMcCabe@aol.com.